1001 Secrets
Every Birder Should Know

By Sharon "Birdchick" Stiteler

Foreword by Bill Oddie

RUNNING PRESS
PHILADELPHIA · LONDON

Books published by Running Press are available at special discounts for bulk purchases in the United
States by corporations, institutions, and other organizations. For more information, please contact the
Special Markets Department at the Perseus Books Group, 2300 Chestnut Street, Suite 200, Philadelphia,
PA 19103, or call (800) 810-4145, ext. 5000, or e-mail special.markets@perseusbooks.com.

ISBN 978-0-7624-4734-3
Library of Congress Control Number: 2012954930

E-book ISBN 978-0-7624-4832-6

9 8 7 6 5 4 3 2 1
Digit on the right indicates the number of this printing

Cover and interior design by Jason Kayser
Edited by Geoffrey Stone
Typography: Avenir, Chronicle, and Giza

Running Press Book Publishers
2300 Chestnut Street
Philadelphia, PA 19103-4371

Visit us on the web!
www.runningpress.com

For Bill. Tolerant, tolerant Bill.

Contents

downy woodpecker

Acknowledgments

There is never enough thanks to give to my non-birding husband, Bill Stiteler. He's put up with my long trips, my babbling about brown birds, bought me so many books and even when my love of birds can appear to trump our relationship or I come home with a new parasite, he is still with me. And he even maintains my birding website. Thank you, Bill, I do love you.

A big thank-you to my editor, Geoffrey Stone, who had to deal with my crazy bird survey and bird festival schedule over deadlines. I am a firm believer that a writer is only as good as her editor and this wouldn't be nearly as fun to read without him.

Another huge thank you needs to go out to Holly Schmidt, who read my blog and got this whole book rolling. Thank you, Holly.

A special thank-you to my agent, Merrilee Heifetz, for sticking with me as an author, even when I drive her nuts.

Other thanks to Brie Anderson, Raul Arias de Para, Tim Appleton, Paul Baicich, Matt Bango, Tracy Bernhardt, Carlos Bethancourt, Trace Beualieu, Mike Bergin, Edward Brinkley, Dougal Q. BunnyPants, Amber Burnette, Dean Capuano, Evan Carrigan, Christopher Ciccone, Richard Crossley, Alex Downie, Rob Drieslein, Dan Dressler, Michele Dupraw, Richard Dupraw, Lang Elliot, Steve Endres, Laura Erickson, Tony Ernst, Roger Everhart, Corey Finger, Ted Floyd, Jason Frederick, Greg Gard, Jeff Gordon, Liz Gordon, Terri Graves, Neil Gaiman, Lorraine Garland, Catherine Hamilton, Carrol Henderson, Steve Holzman, Amy Hooper, Ari Hoptman, Anthony Hertzel, Tammy Holmer, Alvaro Jaramillo, Peter Jones, Steve Kaufer, Kenn Kaufman, Kim Kaufman, Maureen Keefe, T. J. Kudalis, Paul Johnsgard, Randall Kinkor, Nikki Koval, Mark Martell, Jonathan Meyrav, Kirk Mona, Linda Munson, Craig Nash, Hans Newstrom, Mark Newstrom, Frank Nicoletti, Bill Oddie, Jay Ovsiovitch, Peter Perrino, Richard Phillips, Sue Plankis, LeAnn Plinske, Ron Plinske, Ian Punnett, Curt Rawn, Mark Robinson, Larry Sirvio, Lynne Schoenborne, Paul Sedler, Susan Stam, Bill Stiteler Sr. Judy Stiteler, Jenna Strahan-Ouren, Joseph Studnicka, Frank Taylor, Bill Thompson III, Nathan Swick, Clay Taylor, Brian Valentine, Nicole Wagner, Julie Waters, Judy Watson, Susy Woodson, and Julie Zickefoose.

And a very, very special thank-you to Dr. and Mrs. Paul and Judy Strange, you know what you did and who knows where I would be without that. Not a day goes by when I don't think about how fortunate I am because of you.

Oh, yeah and every bird on the planet, thank you to you guys too. You rock. Well, except maybe for that one pelican who threw up on me and gave me pouch lice. You didn't rock nearly as much as the other birds.

Foreword

Proper grown-up, serious, scientific ornithologists are mainly interested in and love to talk and write about BEHAVIOUR. They are generally not that bothered about identifying birds, keeping lists of how many they have seen, or even feeding them. They rarely look at a bird and say "how pretty" or listen to bird song and say "how lovely." They love statistics, especially if they are illustrated by graphs, "tables," numbers, and calculations about "population dynamics." They are not so much bird watchers as bird study-ers, less concerned with what birds look or sound like, than with what they are doing. And whatever they are doing it is called "behaviour." Even if it isn't.

I have spent the last twenty years of my life making wildlife (particularly birds) programs for the BBC, and I have concluded that a large percentage of what a scientist may regard as interesting behaviour is in fact—how can I put this?—bloody boring. A lively commentary—provided by myself—may make it slightly less boring, but a dissertation by an ornithologist will often render it unbearable and—more to the point—unwatchable. Unwatchable does not make good telly.

Throughout my career I have always been guided by this principle: even though I may wish to impart some knowledge or promote some conservation cause, first and foremost I have to make an entertaining show. Whether it is a comedy (I've done that), a panel game (I've done that too), a drama (I've done one), or a documentary about genealogy, archeology, or dinosaurs (I've done 'em all), the aim is the same—to entertain. The ingredients also are the same: drama, humour, tragedy, beauty, spectacle, excitement, witty and articulate words, pleasing or characterful voices, and appropriate music.

So, no place for behaviour!? Oh there certainly is, but let us be honest, when a wildlife film cameraman tells you excitedly that he has got some great "behaviour," what he means is bad behaviour. Birds behaving badly! That's what we want to see. Chasing each other, attacking each other, eating one another. Cameramen will kill for a "kill" or better yet for birds behaving naughtily: flirting, displaying, mounting, doing it. Doing it again. And again. And again. Seriously misbehaving, being unfaithful, promiscuous, and in a few cases downright weird.

But wait, I hear you say or think, "Why is he rattling on about his TV programs when we've never seen them and are prob-ably never likely to?" I'll tell you why. Because in Sharon (Shaz, Birdchick), I recognize a kindred soul. I have only met her once (at a Bird Festival in Israel), but it was immediately clear how much we had in common. For starters, we weren't Scandinavian, which most of the party were. We both lacked inches (in the height department) but carried a small surfeit in other regions. We both talked (maybe too much) and both of us seemed inexorably attracted to the frivolous. True, she was beardless (she still is, as far as I know), and she is obsessively addicted to her smartphone (which I don't even possess). Nevertheless, I think I would go so far as to say that if I were to write a book about birds that was amusing, informative, and sometimes a bit rude, this would be it. In fact, I am a little pissed that I haven't done so. Enjoy.

BILL ODDIE O.B.E.

Introduction

The most important thing you need to know is that bird-watchers are crazy. Most of us are crazy in the good way, a few in the weird way, but at the end of the day, we are all nuts. And that's okay, welcome to the fold!

The second thing you need to know, and chances are good you already do, is that birds are cool and amazing. They come in all shapes, sizes, and brilliant colors, and some even look like they were designed by Dr. Seuss.

Bird-watching is more than a hobby. It's an activity you can enjoy no matter where you travel to on the planet. It's a scavenger hunt, and the objects fly and sometimes change color! It's an adventure.

I once spent money to visit a blind on the side of the Platte River in Kearney, Nebraska. We arrived at 4:30 a.m. on a freezing March morning to sit in a cold dark box covered in frost. As I stood nestling my gloved hands deeper into my pockets, I could hear thousands of sandhill cranes calling on the river in front of us. Gradually, it became brighter as the sun slowly crept toward the horizon. I began to make out actual crane shapes on the water. I could see islands in the center of the river covered in cranes. It was so strange and beautiful to watch forty thousand three-foot-tall lanky birds milling about in front of me.

As it was just bright enough to get photos, a bald eagle flew over the cranes. There was a pause, a silence, and then a *whoosh* sound as forty thousand sets of wings flapped. All the cranes lifted into the air, and each individual trumpeting call of the cranes merged into the sound of a roar. The eagle startled the birds into flight, and the din forced everything out of my head: the cold weather, my lack of coffee, and my shivering toes. In that moment, there was just thousands of cranes and me.

I loved that moment so much, I got a sandhill crane tattooed on my back. Birding doesn't have to take you that far, but it will take you to amazing places.

If you watch birds, you are one of nearly forty-seven million people in the United States who do. Anyone can enjoy birds in their own way from enjoying chickadees flitting from a backyard feeder to counting every bird you see in a year to taking photos that tickle your fancy. No matter how you slice it, birds are fantastic and offer a variety of ways to enjoy their beauty, and they all touch us in some special way.

Watching birds can reveal that you don't just have a backyard, but a live theater version of *National Geographic* playing on a daily basis. I was at a friend's house when I heard a woodpecker screech. In the back of my mind I thought, "Hmm, distressed woodpecker call. Holy cow, distressed woodpecker call!"

I turned to look out the window, and a bird of prey was gliding to the ground with a woodpecker in its talons. When it settled and finished off the bird, I could see it was a small female falcon called a merlin. She had just killed a red-bellied woodpecker that was almost her size. We were sad to see the woodpecker go, but what a treat to see this raptor migrating through and stopping for a meal.

This book is to help you enjoy birds. I want to share with you insights of bird biology and their behavior—the spark that drives many of us to watch them. Most people love listing all the birds that they've seen because at the end of the day, bird-watching is a scavenger hunt where the items fly and sometimes even change color!

But there's so much more to enjoy about birds beyond seeing a new species.

verdin

This book will give you fun facts that not only enhance your watching in the field but that you can share at dinner parties. You can impress your guests by informing them that bluebirds do not have blue pigment in the feathers; their feathers are all black. Or if the mood is right, you can mention that if you even come up face to face with a turkey vulture, never startle it. They vomit as a defense mechanism.

Beyond bird behavior, you can make changes and adjustments to your yard to attract birds and create a better nesting habitat for them. There are better seeds to offer in feeders, but you can also plant conifers for roosting and mountain ash for important fuel for birds like waxwings who do not eat at bird feeders. I'll provide little tips and tricks to increase nesting success of certain species.

You may enjoy birds at home, but consider a trip to see some different species. Watching birds doesn't have to be an expensive trip and often can be combined with a nonbirding spouse's trip. Did you know you could make arrangements to see burrowing owls in Las Vegas? South Padre Island is near the Rio Grande Valley, one of the hottest destinations for bird-watching in North America where green jays and plain chachalacas cavort at feeders. Central Park in New York City is a great birding destination and has hosted such unusual birds as a boreal owl. Being married to a nonbirder, I know some great travel destinations and share them with you here.

I love bird-watching because there's no right or wrong way to do it, and as long as you aren't wiping out a whole species by the way you enjoy birds, do what feels good to you. If you enjoy listing and categorizing every bird you see—that's terrific. If you like to peek out your window and see a chickadee at your feeder—that's great. If you think that red-tailed hawk flying overhead is your spirit guide—more power to you.

Just get out there and watch the birds.

CHAPTER 1

Feeding

Eat Like a Bird

Are you sure you want to eat like a bird? If so, you're eating half your weight in food a day and some of those recipes include rendered beef fat mixed with peanut butter and dried crickets. This chapter gives an overview of foods used to attract birds around the world. From coconuts to grape jelly to mealworms to plantings, you can attract birds in your own backyard. You'll also discover shocking examples of what birds have been documented eating around the globe. Every bird has a dark side!

When traveling, always find out where there are feeding stations. Whether you are a hardcore birder or just a casual observer, it's your best chance to see lots of new birds. This feeder in Panama was a rainbow of birds throughout the day, including this chestnut-headed oropendola and blue-gray tanager.

Attracting Birds

The easiest way to begin watching birds is right outside your home. Whether you live in a remote country village or in the thick of a buzzing metropolis, you can attract birds anywhere. As many species adapt to life with humans and more people create wildlife-friendly habitats, great birds can show up anytime, anywhere.

The secret to any bird feeder's success is mammal proofing. Try to mount bird feeders ten to twelve feet away from trees, fences, shrubs, or your home to prevent critters from jumping on them. Try to mount some sort of baffle or guard like a three-foot-long stove pipe at least five feet up on the pole. This should slow down most nonfeathered guests at the feeder.

Top Bird Feeds

This tufted titmouse is enjoying the most popular birdseed on the planet, the black oil sunflower seed. More birds eat sunflower than any other seed.

Nyjer (also known as niger and thistle) is popular with finches. The seed's small size makes it easy to offer in feeders with tiny slits, reducing the chance of a takeover by larger birds and squirrels. Keep in mind, this seed is no longer desirable to finches if it is six months old, so replace it fairly regularly.

Nuts in or out of the shell are a delight to many species including woodpeckers, nuthatches, chickadees, and jays. Almost as many birds will eat nuts as sunflower, however the squirrels tend to give the birds a run for their money.

Many people assume that attracting sparrows will mean a boring sea of brown, but during migration, sparrows come in unique and fun variations. The Harris's sparrow is very popular with birders because they are distinctive with the black Bluto-like beard. They enjoy white millet scattered on the ground.

Suet is rendered beef fat from the liver of a cow. It can be purchased in raw chunks at the grocery store and some companies sell it in convenient cake form in several flavors including nuts, fruit, and dehydrated insects. Some suets are specially formulated into dough so it can be offered in the warmer months without melting.

Some vegetarians and vegans are not fans of offering suet, since it is made out of animal fat. There are **vegetarian suet pellets** available on the market made from plant fats. It may take some time to get birds used to it, but it is a safe alternative to offer your wild birds.

Fruit is the mainstay of feeders in Central and South America. Birders delight in watching tanagers, oropendolas, and euphonias come in to trays of bananas. Oranges and apples can get the attention of robins, blackbirds, catbirds, mockingbirds, and orioles. Apples need to be secured down and it helps to peal away a bit of the skin, but many thrush species, like the female European blackbird, enjoy apples as much as people do. Coconuts are popular with tits. Hummingbirds will lurk around older fruit, attracted to the tiny insects that are attracted to the rotting fruit.

Jelly is primarily offered to orioles but some finches and sparrows will come in for it too.

Nectar is thought to be primarily for hummingbirds, but sometimes other birds like chickadees, finches, woodpeckers, and even fruit bats will come in for it.

Mealworms have grown exponentially in popularity as a food to offer backyard birds. Not all birds eat seeds. The eastern bluebird, for example, prefers mealworms. This feed allows you to offer a wider variety for a buffet. Since not all people are comfortable handling live mealworms, some companies sell them freeze-dried but they are not as popular with the birds.

Suet cakes made of fat make several birds like these adorable bushtits very happy.

BIRD BUSTING!

Offering rice to birds will not make them explode.
This is an urban legend that has survived for years. Many pet bird owners feed their birds cooked rice as a treat and wild ducks depend on flooded rice fields as a source of food during migration. This story was probably started by brides who found being pelted by rice on their wedding day an unpleasant experience.

Hummingbird nectar is the same in Central America as it is in North America. This white-throated jacobin will sip the same stuff that ruby-throated hummingbirds and rufous hummingbirds drink: 4 parts water 1 part sugar.

BIRD BUSTING!

Nectar for hummingbirds and orioles must be red or orange in color.
It is simply not true that nectar for birds needs to be red or orange. There is even some anecdotal evidence that the red dye could be harmful to birds over time. When offering nectar to orioles, sunbirds, and hummingbirds, avoid using dye in the nectar. Wild nectar is clear. It's the flowers that attract them with their color. The feeders will be bright enough to attract the birds.

The Right Feeder for the Birds

Bird feeders come in hundreds of shapes and styles. All of them will feed birds, but the key to picking out the best bird feeder is to select one that can be cleaned easily. If it doesn't come apart for easy cleaning, it is not worth the money. Keep in mind that not all bird feeders are dishwasher safe, so it's best to plan on cleaning them the old-fashioned way with a bit of elbow grease.

Trays are ideal for larger birds like evening grosbeaks and pine grosbeaks.

Tray feeders will get a bird's attention and are great starter feeders. The disadvantage is that when it rains or snows, the food is exposed to the elements. Some come with a roof to help protect the seed from precipitation.

Wooden feeders are the traditional type of bird feeder that many people gravitate to because that was the kind their grandparents or parents had hanging up. Now you can get

Woodpeckers typically use their stiff tail feathers to hold their bodies up when hanging on the sides of trees. Small cage-style feeders can be difficult for them to feed off of, so you may need to hang it in a way to accommodate all sizes of birds.

those same styles made out of recycled plastic. They clean up easily and they last much longer than the traditional cedar feeders.

Tube-style feeders are a nice, sleek design and easy to hang off a deck or plant hook. Look at the feeding ports closely. Some will have tiny slits meant for finch food, while others will have larger holes for sunflower seed.

Some feeders are made of **mesh** so the birds can cling to the whole tube to work the seeds out. These are especially ideal for woodpeckers, chickadees, nuthatches, and tits.

Suet feeders can be simple cages or logs with holes drilled into them. If you offer suet doughs, you can dish it out onto a tray feeder. If you want to attract larger woodpeckers, you need a large feeder.

Bird Feeding Pro Tips

🪶 Never get too relaxed about mammal-proofing your bird feeders. Where there is a bird feeder, there is a squirrel, rat, or raccoon who will find a way into it.

🪶 Weight-sensitive bird feeders work best to keep squirrels out. They close when a heavy squirrel gets on, but stay open when lightweight birds land on them.

It's important to keep your feeder full. If it goes empty, a bird might decide to move in and use it to raise a family. A house wren attempted to use this metal feeder for a nest. Unfortunately it was a poor choice and the chicks died from overheating because the feeder was not designed with the same ventilation that a proper bird-house requires.

🪶 If the idea of keeping a hummingbird feeder clean is too overwhelming, consider attracting them with nectar rich plants like honeysuckle, salvia, and trumpet vine.

🪶 Never feed bread to ducks and geese in parks. There is no nutritional value and with so many people feeding them, they are fat and plump but not getting the nourishment they need. It's best to avoid feeding them, but if you must, use seed or a nutritional pellet like chick starter.

Starling bills are not good at cracking open seed, so offering food in hard shells will keep them from taking over a feeder.

Birds make a mess under the feeder. You can try offering seeds out of the shell so the birds will not leave empty hulls on the ground, but there will always be some mess. Then there's all the lovely stuff that comes out of the other end of the bird. You can get trays to catch some of it, but at the end of the day, learn to live with a little mess and periodically rake it up.

This young cedar waxwing gulps down a showy mountain ash berry. Waxwings are beautiful birds to have in the yard, but they do not come to feeders. Your only chance of getting their attention is with fruit-bearing trees.

Seed and suet is not the only way to go. Fruit-bearing trees can also bring in birds. Certain trees attract tiny insects in early spring, which are a vital source of food as migrants pass through. Get in touch with your local nursery to find out the best native plants for your area.

Well-manicured lawns are basically green desserts to birds. Yards treated with insecticides lack seed-bearing plants and cannot support a bird, let alone one looking to build a nest. If you have weeds on your lawn, consider it a bonus and use it as a step to get away from grass.

The most important thing you can do for birds is to keep your feeder clean to prevent an outbreak of salmonella or some other illness. If your feeder looks dirty like this goldfinch feeder, take it down, empty it out, and clean it *now*. A mild solution of bleach and water or white vinegar will work well.

The most important thing you can do for birds that come to your feeder is to keep them clean. If the feeder looks nasty to you, chances are it's not all that appealing to birds. Use a mixture of equal parts water and white vinegar or a capful of bleach with a gallon of water to clean your feeders.

Critters will visit your feeders at night. They can be small and relatively harmless like voles and flying squirrels. However, they can also be large and destructive like bears and raccoons that will take feeders away into the woods, never to be seen again.

If you let your cat run around your yard, do not put up a bird feeder. Cats live longer (as do birds) if left indoors.

HUMMINGBIRD NECTAR

4 parts water
1 part sugar

Stir until sugar is dissolved. Use a little hot water to help dissolve the sugar as you add in cool water for the rest. You can make a large batch and store it in the refrigerator for up to two weeks.

Some are tempted to increase the sugar content of this recipe to attract more hummingbirds, but a four-to-one ratio of water to sugar is closer to the sugar content of nectar from flowers. If you do raise it, the birds will dehydrate sooner and visit for shorter periods of time.

Keep in mind that you don't need red dye when making nectar for birds like ruby-throated hummingbirds.

The Palestine sunbird is the Middle East version of a hummingbird and can be taught to visit a nectar feeder. Orioles and woodpeckers will also come in for a sample.

Hummingbirds are only found in North America, Central America, and South America. Do not expect to put up a nectar feeder in Italy and then hope one day that one will fly over the Atlantic to visit. However, nature needs pollinators and birds all over the world will sip nectar, so you just might get a visitor.

SUET RECIPE

1 pound beef suet

1 (16-ounce) jar chunky peanut butter

2 cups cornmeal

1 cup black oil sunflower seeds

I don't recommend making suet in your home. It's an incredibly messy business and a little time consuming, often leaving your home smelling like county fair food. There are several different iterations of suet. One of the most popular to make was developed by writer and artist Julie Zickefoose and affectionately referred to as Zick Dough. That recipe can be found at www.juliezickefoose.blogspot.com/2010/03/zick-dough-improved.html or search for Zick Dough. Here's another popular recipe.

Chop up beef suet into smaller pieces (a meat grinder works well for this if you have one). Place chopped suet into a pot and cook on very low heat until the fat has liquefied. There will be a few chunks that float on top. You can either scrape that off with a spoon or run the fat through a cheesecloth.

Mix the fat with the peanut butter, cornmeal, and sunflower seeds. Some people like to add in other ingredients like dried berries, nuts out of the shell, or oatmeal.

When the mixture is cool, offer it in a suet log, a suet feeder, a tray, or spread it on the side of a tree trunk.

BIRD BUSTING!

Peanut butter will suffocate birds because it gets lodged on the roof of their beaks, blocking their nostrils.

No one has ever studied this and plenty of people offer peanut butter, so if this were an issue, there would be reports of dead birds with peanut butter stuck to their beaks all over the place. If you wish to err on the side of caution, mix cornmeal in with peanut butter to give it a doughier consistency.

Suet is a popular food with any insect-eating bird like black-capped chickadees.

Many think suet is only for winter feeding, but thanks to recipes with corn-meal and oats, it turns suet into a doughy consistency and allows it to be offered year-round, much to the delight of warblers, wrens, thrushes, and even orioles like this altamira oriole.

BASIC BIRDSEED MIX

20 pounds black oil
   sunflower seed
10 pounds safflower or
   golden safflower
10 pounds shelled
   peanuts
5 pounds cracked corn
5 pounds white millet

Most stores offer seed mixes. Some may have different formulas, but really all you need to attract a wide variety of feathered friends to your yard is a sunflower mix. If you are not certain, purchase a mix that is mostly black in color. You can also purchase the ingredients separately and then mix them up at home. If you have birds in your yard that eat seed, they will love this mix.

Place in a large tub and mix with your hands. You can also mix a little bit at a time in a small bowl or bag.

rose-breasted grosbeak
at a peanut feeder

SWEEPLESS MIX

10 pounds hulled sun-
flower seed or
sunflower chips
8 pounds shelled
peanuts
2 pounds cracked corn
1 pound dried berries

If you want to avoid the empty seed shells birds can leave in their wake, try this shell-free mix. Keep in mind that seeds out of the shell are far more expensive than seeds in the shell and if you have starlings, they will chow down on this like senior citizens at an Old-Country buffet on two-for-one night.

Place in a large tub and mix with your hands. You can also mix a little bit at a time in a small bowl or bag.

FINCH MIX

6 pounds nyjer (also
called niger or thistle)
4 pounds extra-fine
sunflower chips
1 pound flax seed

Finches, though small, do not necessarily need small food. However, most tube feeders made for finches have tiny slits for feeding ports so the seed must be tiny in order to fit through there. This helps insure that only finches will come to your feeder, but don't be surprised to find goldfinches hanging out with larger birds to eat black oil sunflower seed. They do have a tendency to be bullied a bit more by larger birds, so a feeder made just for them is ideal.

Place in a large tub and mix with your hands. You can also mix a little bit at a time in a small bowl or bag.

It is possible to go a little nuts when attracting birds and sometimes it's important to take a step back. Some cities have rules about feeding wildlife and, for the most part, they aren't enforced unless someone gets a little nutty with their bird feeding. There are about five news stories a year about someone going to court and being forced to remove their feeders. Don't become that person.

Sheila Lawrence, affectionately referred to as the "Swan Lady," lived on a stretch of the Mississippi River next to a power plant that kept the river open all winter long. As Minnesota was reintroducing the endangered trumpeter swan, a pair showed up one winter, and she offered them ample corn. The next winter, more showed up. After several years of this, fifteen hundred to two thousand trumpeter swans began wintering in the neighborhood.

The area has become a local tourist and bird-watching attraction. However, the Department of Natural Resources (DNR) and other wildlife experts were concerned that if feeding didn't continue or if the river should ever freeze up, an entire population of swans could die. The DNR ordered feeding to be stopped but swans started dying, and the feeding had to be continued at the tune of close to two thousand pounds of corn a day. Wild birds should not be reliant on humans at all.

Another classic example is the "Eagle Lady" in Alaska. Jeane Keane lived in Homer and noticed the bald eagles near her home. She began to put out fish for them and, like the swans, more and more came. At one point, more than two hundred eagles a day were showing up. Sure it can seem cool to have two hundred eagles in the neighborhood, but they loafed on roofs and cars, left an unwelcome mess, and became a general nuisance to many of the residents. After the Eagle Lady died, the town banned the feeding of bald eagles.

BIRD BUSTING!

Will birds die if I stop feeding them?

Healthy birds will not die if you suddenly stop filling the bird feeder. Most birds are smart enough to use several feeding areas on their daily flight path, in case one area stops offering food.

Ten Signs You Need to Cut Back

You know you need to cut back on feeding birds if . . .

1. You have increased the amount of ramen noodles in your diet to afford your birdseed habit.

2. Birdseed and birdseed accessories are more than 20 percent of your credit card debt.

3. Your partner or spouse has said, "It's me or the bird feeder."

4. Your city is considering an ordinance against you.

5. You are convinced that hundreds of birds will die if your feeder goes empty for one day.

6. People refer to you as, the "Bird Lady" or the "Bird Man," even if it's a specific species like, "Purple Martin Man."

7. You find seed or suet stuck in your hair more than three times a week.

8. Both family and neighbors staged an intervention more than once about your bird feeding.

9. Migratory routes have shifted to pass over your yard.

10. A producer from the TV show *Hoarders* has approached you for an interview.

If more than two of these statements apply, you may have a problem. I'm not judging; I'm just pointing out an area in which you may need professional help.

Amazing Things Birds Eat

You've probably heard the phrase "she eats like a bird" used to refer to a thin woman. That's not really true when you really think about what birds eat. Sure, for some it's birdseed, which doesn't seem so filling, but then there are birds like turkey vultures that find a dead beached whale super tasty! Some birds will eat half their weight in food a day during migration. Yikes! Some hummingbirds will eat *three times* their weight in food a day, which is usually sugar water and tiny insects. Oh, the price to pay for having high metabolism!

What some birds really will eat may surprise you. Many know vultures eat carcasses, but so do several other birds. A gray jay feeds off of a deer carcass in this photo. The bird is mainly after the fat. Some deer hunters who live in remote areas will hang out the rib cage or torso for woodpeckers, chickadees, and nuthatches. No doubt, this habit of small birds feeding on carcasses is what inspired people to offer beef suet in their yards.

Laysan albatross mistakenly grab bits of plastic trash on the open ocean instead of fish and feed it to their chicks. One study suggests that over 97 percent of layson albatross chicks have plastic in their stomachs. Some have so much that they are unable to swallow fish and starve to death. Contents include toothbrushes, lighters, plastic toys, and bottle caps. Most of the trash comes from discarded plastic left in streets, which goes to sewers, then to rivers, and then to the oceans. Dispose of plastic properly, even if you live in a landlocked area.

Robert Elner led an international team of researchers who discovered that western sandpipers depend on biofilm, a mucousy layer on top of mud that is created by bacteria and diatoms in seawater. Ew.

American robins, known for eating earthworms and berries, have been documented eating small fish and small snakes.

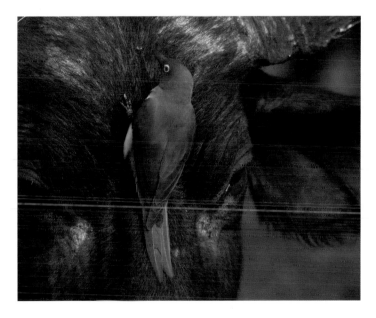

If woodpeckers peck on wood, guess what the red-billed oxpecker pecks on? They are after ticks and insects on large animals.

Osprey are true specialists. Most birds of prey will mix up their diets. Birds that eat mostly other birds will periodically go for a mammal and vice versa. Not the osprey—they only eat fresh fish and nothing else.

The harpy eagle's feet are so huge they resemble the hands of a large man. These formidable birds hunt the tree canopy of the Central American forests for monkeys and have been documented taking sloths.

The oxpeckers' preferred food is blood. They do eat insects but it is usually in the form of blood-bloated ticks. However, they are better known for their habit of pecking open wounds on mammals to get at the blood directly, turning large mammals like impala and cattle into walking bird feeders.

Birds, especially females, need calcium during the breeding season. Ducks will eat snails whole as the shells are a vital nutrient. You can offer crushed eggshells at your own bird-feeding station as well. Many recommend heating crushed eggshells in the oven for ten minutes at 250°F to kill off any salmonella.

BIRD BUSTING!

Is it true that the government is paying off a family that lost their baby because a bald eagle carried it off?

There's a popular urban legend out there that pops up from time to time about a woman who left her four-month-old baby outside on a blanket while hanging laundry on the clothesline. She stepped into her home for just a second and the baby and blanket were gone. A search was conducted to look for the baby and it was never found. But later that summer, Department of Natural Resources (DNR) employees were banding bald eagle chicks and found a diaper and a baby blanket in the nest. The DNR now pays that family to keep them from talking so people won't shoot bald eagles in anger.

Not true. No state organization has that kind of money. And bald eagles can only carry half their weight in flight. They range in size between eight and ten pounds. A four-month-old would be too heavy.

It's a Bird-Eat-Bird World Out There

This merlin grabbed off of a bird feeder a red-bellied woodpecker that is almost the same size as it. It's not always pretty to watch, but you will attract all sorts of birds when you have a good feeding station.

When you have an active bird-feeding station, you will eventually attract predators of the birds visiting like sparrow hawks, Cooper's hawks, and merlins. You can try to have thick brush or bushes for birds to hide in, but keep in mind that birds of prey will hunt these birds regardless of your feeding station. The only thing that's changed is that you have set up a situation so you can watch it.

When peregrine falcons were first reintroduced to the Midwest, researchers lost the first batch of young falcons to great horned owls that ate all the new birds that were put out that first summer.

🪶 Peregrine falcons are bird specialists. Their folk name was the duck hawk for their tendency to go for small waterfowl like teal. The roster of bird parts found in peregrine nests includes rails, grebes, nighthawks, woodcocks, and even parts of herons.

🪶 Greater roadrunners are meat eaters that go for small lizards, mammals, and birds. They have been known to stake out hummingbird feeders to prey on the unsuspecting tiny birds. It's a brutal way to go—they lack the talons of larger birds of prey and instead whack their prey on the ground several times to knock their victims out.

🪶 Thanks to the painting of blue jays raiding a nest and chugging egg yolks like frat boys at a beer bong by John James Audubon, many people do not like them. But it's not just the jays that rob nests! Crows, ravens, and woodpeckers have been known to eat bird eggs too.

🪶 Shrikes have the nickname "the butcher bird" because they prey on large insects like grasshoppers, small mammals, and even small birds. Since they also lack large talons and have a smaller hooked beak, they will impale their prey on barbed-wire fences or thorny bushes and peel off strips of meat. If prey is ample, they will save some food for later and you might find several prey impaled on wire or thorns. This is also known as a shrike, larder, or cache.

🪶 Eastern white pelicans that hang out in St. James Park in London have found a new and unusual food source in the form of pigeons. Though pelicans are known as fish eaters, they will take advantage of available meat in whatever form they can find. There are several videos on the Internet documenting this unusual food gathering technique.

Though loggerhead shrikes will eat grasshoppers and mice, they will occasionally stake out a bird feeder and grab a small bird.

Watering Hole

All birds need water in some form and this purple finch and American goldfinch are as happy to sip from this as they are to nibble at a finch feeder.

Don't forget to add some water to your yard. This is often a great compromise if you live in an apartment or townhome and the building association does not allow bird feeding. Water can be offered in many ways from the traditional birdbath, a fountain, or building a small pond. Every bird, no matter the species, needs water for drinking and for bathing.

If you live in an area with harsh winters, there are heaters or birdbaths with heaters built in that will keep the water open. The temperature will not be like a hot tub, but just warm enough to prevent ice from forming over the top.

Some people like to create large backyard ponds and stock them with fish such as koi. Keep in mind that this may become an unintentional feeder. As herons and egrets grow more accustomed to humans, they will not be able to resist a pond stocked with brightly colored fish that have been trained to come to the surface for food when the water is disturbed.

Fountains are especially handy for attracting birds. Simply setting out a dish of water doesn't always attract the birds right away, but the sound of running water gets their attention.

The secret to a proper birdbath is to keep it shallow. Small birds like finches and chickadees only need about a half-inch of water to get a good bath. So unless you want crows and hawks using it exclusively, get a small bath.

Hummingbirds have such tiny feet that they cannot walk on them. Their preferred method is to zip back and forth under a sprinkler to get a good shower.

Birds love the sound of water and the bushtits love this dripper.

immature red-tailed hawk

BIRD BUSTING!

Can a hawk, owl, or eagle kill and fly off with my pet?

Understand that if you have a pet that is under ten pounds, it was designed to have a very important place on the food chain and you should be responsible for it out in the wild. A great horned owl and red-tailed hawks only weigh about three pounds and can't carry too much weight. But a desperately starving bird or young bird may try. It's rare for birds of prey to go for pets; your small dog, cat, or pet rabbit is in far more danger of being eaten by coyotes than a bird of prey.

Vacation Ideas

Bird-feeding stations are a fun and easy way to enjoy birds, whether you are a beginning bird-watcher, photographer, or even a hardcore birder looking to add a few species to the day's list. This is far easier than looking for birds while being pelted by mosquitoes, chiggers, and ticks. It's simple enough to use the Internet to search out local nature centers with feeding stations set up in your area, but there are also some fantastic opportunities outside of your home.

Laguna Atascosa National Wildlife Refuge (NWR)
South Texas is a bird-watching paradise and everyone should have it on their bucket list. Unless you plan for a long stay, it can be a challenge to fit in all the birding areas. Not only can you relax on a bench and take in spectacular birds like altamira orioles, plain chachala-cas, and green jays, but sometimes Mexican birds sneak across the border and you might be rewarded with a clay-colored thrush. Laguna also offers a wildlife drive, which can yield crested caracaras, roadrunners, and apolomado falcons. Its close proximity to South Padre Island makes it a great destination when a vacation is not centered entirely on watching birds.

Delaware Bay/Bombay Hook NWR
This is not a bird-feeding station in the traditional sense—no one is putting out bags of seed or jars of peanut butter. However, lovely salmon-colored shorebirds called red knots gather by the thousands to load up on horseshoe crab eggs to fuel their return journey to the tundra for breeding. It is estimated that it's possible to see 90 percent of the world's pop-ulation of red knot in a day. This is especially critical as overharvesting of horseshoe crabs as conch bait has reduced their population by over half since the 1980s.

Alaska Chilkat Bald Eagle Preserve
This forty-eight thousand-acre preserve protects a natural salmon run, which attracts one of the largest concentrations of bald eagles. Designated parking areas allow for easy viewing of three thousand bald eagles from October through January. The rest of the year, the eagles number between two hundred to three hundred.

CHAPTER 2

Bird Real Estate

We all know birds need food and water to survive but they are also in dire need of space for nesting and roosting. These are two very different activities, and though birds are known for creating amazing and even elaborate nests, most birds use nests for child rearing and not sleeping.

A field biologist points to a Savannah sparrow nest on the ground for photo documentation. Don't worry if you have touched a nest; birds will still return to it.

Nests can be anywhere including the tops of trees, on top of football stadium lights, water towers, and chimneys. Not only will they be high, but they can be low too. Prairie species conceal their nests in grasses, and some like kingfishers even nest underground. Birds take advantage of a good resource when they can find it. Some birds have an easier time finding shelter than others, and we can help them along by providing housing and nesting material.

Birds that build cup nests like this American robin only use them for nesting. They do not live in them year-round.

In warmer months, birds will create nests to raise their chicks. Early on in incubation, one parent may sleep in the nest. As the chicks grow, there may not be enough room for a parent in the nest and they must sleep nearby. Nests vary from species to species; some birds are loners who prefer the dark recesses of a cavity in a tree trunk, others are colony nesters who barely make an impression in the sand and lay their eggs within inches of other nests.

BIRD BUSTING!

If I build a birdhouse, birds will come.
Not always. Keep in mind that habitat is a big factor in a bird's choice to use a nest box. You may want an eastern bluebird in your backyard and have the best house for one, but if your yard is heavily wooded, this open field–loving species will ignore it. Also, know what birds are in your area. Blue tits are cute birds and often pictured on packaging for birding products. However, if you live in Kentucky, your chances of attracting this bird are astronomical because this bird lives in Europe.

Crazy Nests

Bushtits are one of several bird species that weave hanging-basket–type nests.

Orioles, oropendolas, and caciques are among birds that make pendulous nests, woven baskets that hang on the ends of branches. Some say they resemble a certain piece of the male anatomy. Some orioles, like the Baltimore oriole, weave shorter baskets close to the branch; others, like altamira orioles, weave long pendulous baskets for their young. Oropendolas and caciques make deep baskets too, but unlike orioles, they do so in large, noisy colonies.

Southern yellow-billed hornbill males deliver mud and droppings to females who seal themselves into their nest cavities to rear their young. They leave an opening just large enough for the males to slip food through.

Some birds build nests that stay in families for generations. The sociable weaver in southwestern Africa creates gigantic structures made of coarse, dry grass that are used and added to every year, so long as the tree can hold it. There are some sociable weaver nests that are said to be over a century old.

Eagles constantly renovate their nests and make them larger over several years. An average bald eagle nest is usually four to five feet in diameter, and about six to nine feet deep. There was a record-breaker in Florida who had a nest that was over nine feet wide and over twenty feet deep. The weight of the nest was almost three tons.

Hornbill females like their privacy when nesting, so much so that they build their own little fortresses of solitude in a tree cavity. Once a nesting site has been selected, she will plaster up the opening, leaving only a tiny slit large enough for the male's beak to slip through and deposit food. She will remain inside for about three months. When the young are ready to leave and learn to fly, she will break open the wall. Depending on the species of hornbill, the plaster can be made of mud, resin, masticated bark and food, or even droppings.

Some species of swallows construct nest cups out of mud and saliva. Imagine making your precious newborn baby a crib from mud and your saliva.

Some birds apparently build tasty nests. The edible-nest swiftlet constructs a nest entirely out of its gummy saliva that is harvested and used to make bird's nest soup. This is such a prized delicacy that people in Borneo try to make housing for them so they can sell the nests.

Bald eagles construct huge nests. The constant additions can be too much for the tree, and after several years it may come crashing down. Eagles usually have a spare nest ready to go in the territory just in case this happens.

In North America, there is a type of warbler called an ovenbird that builds its nest on the ground. The nest is protected by a roof made of leaves, twigs, and grasses that keeps rain out and hides the contents from predators.

Another type of ovenbird is not related to the North American warbler and resides in South America. It will construct an earthen dome on tree branches, telephone posts, or window ledges. The birds take months creating the domed nest with mud, dung, and even straw. Once hardened by the sun, the nest is almost impossible for a natural predator to destroy.

Monk parakeets, also known as Quaker parrots, are native to South America but have established colonies in North America and Europe as birds have been released. The birds build large twiggy configurations that can hide nest holes for several pairs.

In Africa, the hamerkop makes a huge nest structure that can hold over ten thousand pieces of material. Mostly made of sticks, the hamerkop will not hesitate to add anything it can get its bill on—including plastic. The structure includes a base, roof, and tunnel. The nests are so huge that other bird species like pigeons and mynahs may build their nests on the outside of it.

As pet birds are let loose in the wild monk parakeets are expanding their breeding range. They live in large colonies and love old buildings to create their large stick nests. Brooklyn hosts a huge colony in Green Wood Cemetery.

Subterranean Nesters

Isabelline wheatears nest underground by taking over old rodent nests.

Many birds like woodpeckers will peck holes in trees to use for a nest, but a few birds actually nest in the ground. The advantage to nesting underground is that you are hidden from predators. Sooty shearwaters go the extra mile and only visit their burrows at night to prevent predators from discovering the location of the nest.

Leach's storm petrels also nest underground, and like shearwaters, they avoid the burrow during the day and even on moonlit nights, so predators will not find the nest.

Burrowing owls nest underground, sometimes taking a burrow in a prairie dog or other ground squirrel colony. One of their defenses when disturbed in the burrow is to make a sound similar to a rattlesnake to encourage potential predators to go away.

Puffins live in burrows underground.

Kingfishers will dig out a
burrow in the side of a stream.
A pied kingfisher burrow
can be five feet deep.

Tenacious Nesters

Rock pigeons are survivors and have spread worldwide. One of the secrets of their success is their ability to nest anywhere and make nests out of anything, including nails or spent bottle rockets. Spikes are often used to keep them from roosting on buildings, but some pigeons have used the spikes as a base for a nest.

House wrens build several nests in any cavity they find in their territory and only raise chicks in one. Some will have as many as six nests, which is amazing when you consider that the house wren is less than five inches long. The advantage is that when a predator enters the wren's territory, they will defend one of the empty nests, using it as a decoy so the predator will not raid the one full of eggs or chicks.

House wrens use whatever tactic they can to use a nest box. If another species has eggs in a box they want, a wren will go inside when the nest is unattended and poke holes in the eggs to prevent them from hatching and encouraging the original tenants to try and nest elsewhere.

Cactus wrens will also destroy the eggs in the nests of other birds near their territory. They also build the Fort Knox of nests by constructing it in the middle of a thorn bush or, like their name suggests, a cactus.

BIRD BUSTING!

Birds live in their nest year-round.
Not really. A nest is used as a nursery for raising chicks. Birds may use some cavities or nest boxes from time to time for sleeping, but most nests are only used to raise young.

Cactus wren protect their young by building nests in cacti or other thorny plants.

Barely-There Nests

Mourning doves build surprisingly haphazard nests of a few twigs anywhere they can. Though the nests can easily fall apart, they can regroup and renest quickly.

Pelicans live in large colonies, usually on islands and often mixed with other species like herons, gulls, terns, or cormorants. The birds might gather a few sticks, but otherwise plop their eggs right on the ground.

Piping plovers make a scrape in the sand on beaches and they may surround it with pieces of shell, but they mostly rely on the camouflage of the eggshells to hide their nests. All piping plovers are endangered, and there's a big effort to raise awareness on beaches to not tread on their nests and young.

BIRD BUSTING!

If a bird nests on my porch, my coming and going will cause it to abandon its chicks.

Some birds make an informed decision when they nest on a porch. Perhaps they realize that some predators do not like to come near humans and are willing to risk people constantly being around. You may have to duck a few times, but for the most part, birds and people can cohabitate fairly well.

Some Birds Build No Nest at All

Unlike North American cuckoos, European cuckoos do not build their own nests, but lay their eggs in other birds' nests. Sometimes the birds are a third of the size of the cuckoo.

Cowbirds in the Americas also do not build their own nests, but will lay an egg in another bird's nest. Female brown-headed cowbirds have been documented monitoring where eggs have been laid. If the cowbird egg is removed from the host nest or if the host bird builds a new nest on top of the compromised one, she will return to the nest and destroy all the eggs by smashing them with her bill.

The beautiful white fairy tern simply lays her egg on a branch without any additional twigs, moss, or fur. Though this keeps it safe from ground predators, some aerial predators will try to find a way to knock the egg off the branch, causing it to break when it falls and providing a satisfying and nourishing meal.

You would think that if you are nesting in a frozen place like the Antarctic you would want a large nest to incubate an egg, but there's a lack of nesting material to be found. Emperor penguins build no nest at all. Since even a few seconds on the ice could kill the chick growing inside the shell, they balance the egg on the tops of their toes and use their great layers of fat and feathers to keep the egg warm until it hatches.

Potoos are an awesome family of birds. If someone ever says, "Hey, I got a lead on a potoo, want to go see it?" say yes! Their plumage makes them look like a broken branch. Because a nest would mess up their great camouflage lifestyle, the female lays her egg on the branch and raised her young there.

Squatters

Usually great horned owls will take over a hawk nest in a wooded area. However, this one chose to take over an osprey nest out in the open in Florida. The owls in Florida must like to experiment. A few years ago, a pair raised their young in a large planter on the ground outside of the Brevard County Commission.

Many species of owls do not build their own nest but take over an old nest. Some are cavity nesters and will take over a woodpecker cavity. Others, like great horned owls, usurp old hawk, squirrel, or even eagle nests.

House sparrows are very aggressive to other species, even birds twice their size. If a pair decides that they want a cavity that is already in use, they will push out eggs or in some cases, kill the young or even an adult, by piercing the back of the skull with their large, thick beak. Sometimes the sparrows do not even bother to remove the bodies and will build their nest on top of the carnage.

Starlings are another aggressive species. They like to nest in cavities pecked out by woodpeckers, but their beaks are too soft to peck open a hole. In North America, they have been documented chasing off a northern flicker after a nest cavity has been completed.

Nest Maintenance

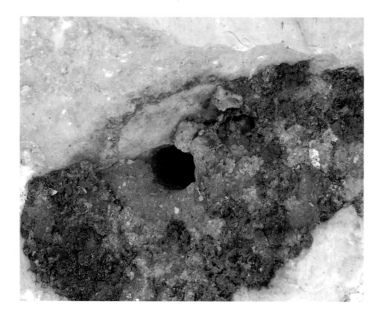

Rather than pecking into a tree like other nuthatches, rock nuthatches construct their own cavities on cliffs. If you look closely at this photo, you'll see crushed beetle bodies surrounding the entrance. This is believed to be a tactic to combat nest parasites.

After the nest is built, adults may make additions. Sometimes sticks need to be added for maintenance after a storm, but some birds make additions in the form of home security.

Unlike other nuthatches, the rock nuthatch builds its own cavity on the side of a cliff instead of excavating a cavity in a tree. After the nest is complete, the birds will grab beetles and squish them around the entrance. The exact reason isn't known but speculation is that it serves as either a predator deterrent or insect repellant.

Many species of raptor will drop off branches with fresh leaves on them right into their nests. Perhaps the leaves selected might have an insect repellent quality to them but not all scientists agree. Some think it might communicate to rivals that this nest is occupied and maintained, so please stay away.

The Art of Bird Housing

A great way to enjoy birds in the yard and share them with kids is to put up bird housing. Birdhouses come in a variety of shapes and sizes, some are single-family homes, and others are large, multiunit apartment buildings. These types of man-made structures appeal to cavity nesting birds, ones that would naturally use a hole in a tree in the wild. Birds that build cup nests like cardinals or mistlethrushes will not use them. However, chickadees, bluebirds, wrens, and house sparrows will.

Hanging plastic gourds are popular with purple martins.

Sometimes your home may offer desirable housing for birds unintentionally. Holiday wreaths or decorative garlands left out too long may get the attention of robins and mourning doves. Once the bird is nesting, you cannot legally move the nest until the chicks leave the nest (usually in about a month's time).

Hanging flower baskets are especially attractive to house finches and Carolina wrens. If you are concerned about watering your plants if there is a nest inside, you can try to carefully water around the nest (the parents may chirp at you but that would be the worst of it; some will even stay put in the nest). Some people will transfer the nest to a plastic cream cheese container with holes poked in the bottom for drainage and place it in the basket. It's usually easier to water around the nest that way.

This Anna's hummingbird chose to use a garden spinner for her nest. Hummingbirds usually make their nests in the crotch of tiny branches, but they will sometimes use plant hooks or light fixtures as well. Their nests are about the size of a quarter and hard to spot. The female makes the nests out of spiderwebs and lichen.

BIRD BUSTING!

You need to change the nesting material on a regular basis in a nest box. No, do not do this. Some people advise switching out nest material when the birds have chicks, but this is invasive and unnecessary. It's fine to check on a nest box once or twice a week and maybe take a peek. It is a good idea to remove nesting material after the baby birds fledge to encourage birds to go for a second brood in a season. However, birds will not rebuild a nest on a daily or weekly basis. If you are changing nesting material while the chicks are in the nest, you are treating wild animals as pets and you need to take a step back. Birds need us to provide a safe habitat, not to provide maid service.

How to Select a Good Birdhouse

Whether purchasing a nesting box or building your own, there are some common factors that all great birdhouses share. Bird housing comes in all shapes and sizes, but even a decorative house can be made in a safe and effective way for nesting birds.

The best birdhouses are made of sturdy natural materials like cedar. Be wary of plastic or metal housing, it may get too hot for eggs or chicks to survive if placed in direct sun. Not all plastic and metal houses are bad, but make sure the walls are not too thick (a maximum of one inch if wood and three-quarters of an inch if plastic. And never go thicker than aluminum sheeting for metal).

Good birdhouses will have ventilation holes. If the nest box doesn't have proper ventilation, then it is an unsafe house.

Small drainage holes should be included in the floor of the nest box.

The house should easily open in some fashion so it can be cleaned out. Some have a sliding wall; others require you to use a screwdriver in order to open it. If you can't easily open a nest box, do not buy it.

The best birdhouses are held together with screws or nails. Nest boxes that are held together with glue or staples are at great risk of coming apart in rainy conditions.

For smaller birds, the floor of the nest box next to the entrance should be at least five inches deep. You can go a bit deeper, but don't go too deep because the young birds have to get out when they are learning to fly and you don't want to make it too hard for them.

Single-Family Dwellings

The size of the entrance hole on a nest box can help you attract specific species. Some people may only want tiny birds; others may not care who builds a nest in the box, so long as it has feathers. Here are some guides for different bird species. Remember, regardless of the size of the entrance, you need to have the correct habitat for the birds you want and live in the country where these birds breed.

violet-green swallow

1-Inch Entrance Hole

This is an ideal entrance for house wrens, blue tits, coal tits, and marsh tits. Keep in mind that if you live in Europe, you will not have wrens.

1⅛-Inch Entrance Hole

This will work to allow in a little bit larger birds like black-capped chickadees, Carolina chickadees, great tits, tree sparrows, and pied flycatchers.

1¼-Inch Entrance Hole

This size will allow more species including Carolina wrens, white-breasted nuthatches, Eurasian nuthatches, and house sparrows.

1¾-Inch Entrance Hole

This size is attractive to eastern bluebirds, western bluebirds, tree swallows, violet-green swallows, and all of the previous species. There will be a lot of competition for this nest box.

4-Inch-Wide and 3-Inch-Tall Oval Entrance Hole

If you are looking for bigger birds, this is the way to go. This is the entrance for a wood duck or hooded merganser, but you can sometimes get surprises like screech owls, northern saw-whet owls, American kestrels, or northern flickers.

The key to getting this large nest box to work is to place a fresh bedding of cedar chips in the bottom of the box every spring. The box needs to simulate an old woodpecker hole in a natural tree cavity. In the wild, an old tree cavity would have lots of woodchips at the bottom from woodpeckers, so a fresh nest box needs that to be added.

Since this box is for a larger bird, the box should be much larger than one built for small birds. The entrance hole should be at least sixteen inches above the floor of the box. Because baby ducks will have to climb out the day they hatch, the walls should be rough, not smooth. Some boxes even have grooves carved in or hardware cloth attached to the wall under the entrance hole to make crawling out of the box easier.

6-Inch-Wide Oval or Square Entrance Hole

This is an entrance ideal for barn owls and will hopefully prevent larger owls from taking it over.

Multiunit Housing

Birdhouses with small entrance holes that are 1¼ inch are meant for house sparrows. Once they move in, they will not let any other species in.

Purple martins are a popular bird to attract in North America because they will nest in large nest boxes. These loud, boisterous birds are valued for their insect eating ability and elegant beauty. Houses can be as small as eight rooms or as large as 620 compartments. The houses can be made of wood, aluminum, or even gourds, and the entrance hole should be 1¾ inches in diameter.

Good realty is at a premium and males like this purple martin will fight vigorously for a good home.

Housing Pro Tips

Even though it's possible for cavity-nesting waterfowl like wood ducks and hooded merganser chicks to jump from a nest that is fifty feet up in a tree, a nest box is easier to clean out in the fall if it is only six to ten feet high on a post.

You can reduce the chance of predators likes snakes, foxes, raccoons, and cats from climbing up and eating the eggs and chicks inside a nest box if you put it on a pole and put a three-foot-long stove pipe about five feet up on the post. It makes it almost impossible for predators to climb. Some people will also grease the pole to prevent predators, but that can wear off in the rain or with a tenacious climber.

If cats regularly prowl your yard, do not set up nest boxes. The young learning to fly will be easy chew toys.

Some people may put out a nest box with a tiny hole for titmice but a woodpecker or squirrel may decide to make the hole larger. It is possible to find metal frames that you can screw on to the outside of the nest box to prevent other species from making the hole larger. Look for it wherever wild bird products are sold.

Most birds like to build their nests in low-traffic areas. For the best chances of attracting feathered tenants, don't place bird housing next to a bird feeding station.

Some species will nest together peacefully. For example, bluebird houses are prized by many species and competition for a bluebird nest box is high. By putting up houses in pairs, a bluebird pair might take one and a family of tree swallows or chickadees might take the other. Competition for food will be slim, and the birds will defend the territories together.

After the nesting season is finished, either take the nest box down or leave one wall open to the elements to discourage mice from moving in over the winter.

Avoid placing a nest box near bedroom windows. Singing males like to get a start in advertising their territory in song before dawn. When the chicks hatch, they will beg for food before dawn as well. You may find the noise an unwelcome alarm clock.

Blue tits are the European counterpart to chickadees and an example of a bird that will use a nest box.

Think Outside the Nest Box

NEST PLATFORMS

Osprey like a nest with a clear view on all sides. When a new platform is set up, you can encourage osprey interest by adding in a few sticks.

Some birds like something flat to lay down sticks for their homes. If you have a home near a large body of water, you can try your hand at putting up an osprey nesting platform. Keep in mind that this species likes to have a clear view on all sides of the nest. You can find osprey towers as high as two hundred feet or as low as ten feet, but the one thing in common is that there is nothing higher than the platform within one hundred feet.

Floating platforms can be made to encourage loons to nest on a lake. This is especially ideal for lakes with a lot of human shore traffic, or lakes that have frequent fluctuations in water height.

Towers have been erected for herons too. These colony-nesting birds build shallow nests and when their rookeries have been destroyed from a tornado, telephone poles with several platforms attached have been used as a replacement.

This is an artificial heron rookery used by great blue herons in Utah. Note the smaller box attached to one of the poles. That is a barn owl nest box. They are not predators of herons and can coexist peacefully.

Small ledges and platforms can be built to encourage birds that make cup nests to build on certain areas of your home. This is handy if you have a bird that has decided to build on a light fixture and you would prefer it move to a different spot. Nesting ledges attract doves, robins, wrens, thrushes, and even swallows.

FALSE CHIMNEYS

Chimney swifts were an abundant city bird, using chimneys for raising families and, in the case of large industrial chimneys, using them as a roosting area during migration. Because chimney construction and use has changed radically since the 1980s, this valuable insect-eating bird is in decline. There are groups like the Driftwood Wildlife Association dedicated to promoting awareness about chimney swifts. They offer books and plans for individuals or communities to construct false chimneys on roofs or in yards to provide nesting habitat for these amazing insect-eating birds that look like flying cigars. If you are looking for a unique and weird birdhouse for your roof or your garden, this is it.

ROOST BOX

A new trend is to offer a box for some species to sleep or roost in during the winter months. Some cavity-nesting birds will form loose, mixed flocks in winter as they forage and will use the same cavity for sleeping at night, using the shared body heat for additional warmth. These roosting boxes have the entrance hole placed on the bottom of the box to make it less desirable for mice to use as a nesting box.

Large wood duck boxes can also be used for winter roosting spots by small owls. On sunny days, the owls will perch at the opening for warmth. In spring, when you are prepping the box for use by ducks, you might find owl pellets inside and figure out what the tiny owls were eating.

UNINTENTIONAL NESTS

Sometimes birds build nests in an inconvenient place for us: over porch light fixtures, flower baskets, right over the front door, inside work boots, or in rare cases, hawks have built nests on decks while homeowners were away on vacation. Some people love the company; others don't care for protective parents that dive at heads or the excessive poop the young ones create. If this is happening in your home, remove the nest right away, before there are eggs. Once a female has laid her eggs, it is illegal in most circumstances to remove the nest. Also, once a bird has successfully nested in a place, they will come back and do it again. If you have a case of a colony of swallows building mud nests on a wall, you may have to remove attempts to rebuild several days in a row. Think about it: birds live in the wild. They've dealt with stormy weather and wind knocking down nests for a lot longer than they've dealt with humans.

Please understand that in the cases of lone-nesting families of small birds like robins, tits, chickadees, wrens, and finches, the whole nesting process from nest building to the young leaving the nest is finished in the space of a month. That's not a long time, and it's a great way to watch nature live and in-person. It's also a lovely way to introduce kids to the joys of our feathered neighbors.

CONTROVERSIAL TENANTS

In North America, house sparrows and European starlings are problem birds. They are not native to the continent, and they will drive out native birds from nest boxes and have been a cause for decline in some species like purple martins and bluebirds. Many people will go to great lengths to avoid them by designing nest boxes they cannot fit into, or in some cases, trapping and killing them. It is legal in the United States to dispose of nonnative bird species, so long as you do it in a way that doesn't kill native birds.

However, in the United Kingdom where house sparrows are native, the population has plummeted. Some of the decline is attributed to a change in agricultural practices, but the urban sparrow population has declined by over 60 percent and the cause is not known. Because of this alarming drop, the house sparrow is now red-listed as a high conservation concern by the Royal Society for the Protection of Birds in Europe.

People who enjoy nesting birds love to share that passion with others and especially want to make sure other people are doing it in the best way for the birds. Many species that use nest boxes have garnered their own fan clubs that hold annual conventions and publish their own magazines and newsletters. To get the latest information on providing the best nesting habitat on certain species, check out these clubs:

The **Purple Martin Society**'s main goal is to educate the public, offer tips for new "landlords," house designs, product recommendations, and forums for in-depth martin discussion. www.purplemartins.com

The **North American Bluebird Society** was started in the 1970s as a means of connecting bluebird landlords and helping this species in decline. Thanks to some of their birdhouse changes and monitoring, bluebird numbers across the United States have expanded. Some birders like to speak of how many birds are on their list, bluebird people like to say how many young fledged from their trails in a year. www.nabluebirdsociety.org.

The **Barn Owl Trust** is essentially to protect the barn owl's habitat. Like other nesting groups, they want to make sure nesting sites are occupied frequently, housing is safe, and the nest boxes are properly mounted for the owls. Though this group is located in the United Kingdom, barn owls are found on several continents and the trust's information can be helpful no matter where they are found. www.barnowltrust.org

Though many people associate Ducks Unlimited with hunting, they are all about creating better nesting habitats for birds like blue-winged teal. They are a great resource for people who want to create a better duck nesting habitat on their property. Visit www.ducks.org.

eastern bluebird

ENCOURAGE THE BIRD-HOUSING MARKET

Construction material is just as important as offering the housing. There are all sorts of items you can find around your home or purchase to put out for birds. Natural fibers work best and will handle being out in all kinds of weather.

If you put out string, twine, or yarn for birds, cut it into small strips, roughly six inches long. Long materials run the risk of getting caught on branches. Even worse, birds get tangled in them, and it's a slow death of starvation for them if no one intervenes.

Dryer lint may have residue buildup from detergents and fabric softener. No one knows if this is good for baby birds or not, so avoid offering dryer lint as construction material.

Pet fur, feathers, hair, and raw cotton are all great items to set out for birds.

Even if you don't want to put items like hair and pet fur out in your yard, birds may find useful fibers to use from plantings in your yard. Some birds use lichen, some use spiderwebs, others even use shed snakeskin.

This chestnut-sided warbler is using natural plant fiber for nest construction.

Vacation Ideas

Griggsville, Illinois, aka the Purple Martin Capital of the World

Purple martins are large insect-eating swallows. Some literature suggests that they eat quite a few mosquitoes, which is what led the town of Griggsville to offer the largest subsidized bird housing in the nation. The series of martin houses stacked on poles offer over five hundred nest cavities for these insectivores. I can't guarantee that you won't be bitten by mosquitoes, but you will be bowled over by the size and sound of this colony.

Gatorland, Orlando, Florida

This originally started as a preserve for alligators, but the breeding marsh soon attracted the attention of herons, ibises, egrets, spoonbills, and storks and now has a large rookery of wading birds. You have to give the birds credit for this, no ground predator is going to come near that nesting colony with over one hundred alligators swimming in the surrounding waters. This is a great treat for a casual day trip for birds that are big, colorful, and easy to see.

Cape Kidnappers, New Zealand

If you don't have too sensitive of a nose, this is one of the craziest nesting encounters you can have in your life. These elegant birds lay eggs amidst thousands of other gannets, so you can get great photos and literally be mere feet from baby fish-eating birds.

CHAPTER 3

Great Adaptations

When you think about it, birds have the ultimate freedom, living outdoors, being able to survive on their wits and their ability to find food and fly. Part of the reason is that everything they need to survive is right there on their body—from beak to feathers to nails.

Beaks

🌾 Birds do not have teeth or lips. Instead they have a hard substance similar to our fingernails that constantly grows from their faces. Beaks can be used for many purposes—from eating to grabbing to building. Some birds have bill deformities that are not well understood.

🌾 Bird beaks come in all shapes and sizes, from the barely-there nighthawk beak; to the long, curved curlew beak; to the ginormous huge toucan beak. Some deformities occur. In black-capped chickadees and crows in south-central Alaska deformities have been documented at an alarming rate in the last twenty years. Some studies suggest that 7 percent of the chickadee population has deformed overgrown beaks. Their beaks continue to grow faster than their daily activity can wear them down. It is not known what causes overgrown beaks in wild birds.

🌾 Each bird beak has a purpose and has evolved over the years to help that bird carve out a niche of survival in the food chain.

🌾 Watch the birds at your feeder and their beaks will tell you a lot about what they eat. Cardinals and rose-breasted grosbeaks have thick bills, ideal for shredding hard husks off seeds. Starlings have a soft bill that cannot remove the shells. But they have strong muscles for opening their beaks and will use it to sift through empty shells looking for an already shelled seed.

🌾 Most birds have nostrils where the beak connects to the face. This is called a cere and in some species, it will even change color during the breeding season. The kiwi's nostrils are all the way at the tip of the beak.

Black skimmers have a very unique bill. The bottom mandible is much longer than the top, and as their name suggests, the birds fly and dip the lower mandible into the surface of the water. When they detect something by touching it, the bill slams shut.

Should you use "bill" or "beak" when referring to birds? Originally, "beak" was the term for the hooked bill on birds of prey, but nowadays it can be used interchangeably with "bill."

It is thought that woodcock beaks are incredibly sensitive to earthworms and the beak can sense their vibrations in the ground.

It helps to think of certain beaks as utensils. Herons use a chopstick style to grab fish and frogs from the water, while hawks use their sharp beak like a knife to tear off pieces of flesh.

Falcons have a distinct notch on the top part of their beak that is perfect for snapping the small spine of its prey. They are one of the few predators to make sure prey is actually dead before they begin eating it.

Many species of waterfowl like ducks, swans, and geese have little ridges along the upper mandible of their beaks that allows them to filter out water when they grab food underwater.

Cormorants or shags have hooks at the tips of their beaks, helping to secure slippery fish when hunting underwater.

Crossbills have a unique beak where both ends cross in the front. This unique design allows them to wedge the beak into pinecones, pry them apart, and use their tongue to access the nut on the inside.

In Hawaii the ʻakiapōlāʻau is a tiny finch-like bird that has one of the crazier beaks out there. The bottom mandible is hard and used to chip at wood and bark. The top is long and curves downward. The bird cannot peck with the top part, but uses it as a probe to get at grubs.

Nightjars have tiny beaks that don't match their huge mouths. The beak looks like a tiny little nib, but when the birds fly at night with their mouths open, you can see the mouth opens to about one-third the size of the bird's head.

The current record holder for the longest straight bill belongs to the Australian pelican at 18.5 inches. However, if you measure longest bill relative to body length, that goes to the sword-billed hummingbird with a body that is 5.5 inches long with a 7-inch-long beak.

Tests performed on toucans show that their huge bill can be used to release excess heat from their bodies.

Note the ridges on the upper mandible of this trumpeter swan. They help filter water out after they grab vegetation under the water's surface.

Crazy Tongues

If you ever have a chance to see woodpeckers being banded, ask if you can see the tongue, and you'll note that the tip is hard with little spikes. If you are a grub, death by woodpecker is a gruesome way to go.

Woodpeckers have a hard spear-like tip on the ends of their tongues. Tiny spikes facing the back of their mouth cover it. The tongue is also very long; it wraps around the woodpecker's head and can extend three times the length of the beak. They use this to probe inside tight holes and spear grubs and insects.

Birds of prey have a spike on their tongues that faces the back of their mouths and helps send chunks of meat down their throats.

Not that you'll ever be close enough to see it, but hummingbirds have one of the stranger tongues out there. The tongue is actually forked like a snake's tongue and covered in very tiny fringy extensions called lamellae. When the tongue is extended, the forks separate and the little lamellae flail. The hummingbird then rolls it all in with nectar they sip from flowers.

Digestive Adaptations

Do you see the yellow bulge this crested caracara is preening around? This is a full crop; this bird had eaten very well right before this photo was taken.

If you are going to have a life on the go and in many cases, up in the air, you need a digestive tract to help make that happen. Most birds have a crop, a little storage pouch to hold food before it can be digested. When they feed their young, the food comes out of the crop. Jays will come to feeders and gather several seeds and fly away to hide them into a cache. Some jays will have a Dolly Parton look to them when they pack their crops full of corn or peanuts.

Since birds do not have teeth, they need something to help them "chew" up their food. They have this in the form of a gizzard, which helps them grind up food. Species that eat a lot of hard seeds will consume gravel and grit to aid in the grinding process.

Some birds have a gular pouch, a patch of skin between the lower mandible of the beak and the neck. Some species like pelicans and cormorants have an exaggerated pouch and that can be used to store food.

Not every bird can digest everything it swallows. The undigested material will form a pellet that the bird coughs up. This is mostly associated with birds of prey, but several species can produce pellets including gulls, flycatchers, and chickadees. Pellets can contain feathers, fur, exoskeletons of insects, seed hulls, or fish scales.

Pellets from large hawks and eagles can be easily found in the wild. Did you know you can identify whether a hawk or an owl has coughed up the pellet you found? Look for bones. Hawks, eagles, and falcons tend to rip up prey and eat mostly meat. Their stomach acids are strong and can digest most pieces of bone they swallow. Owls tend to swallow prey whole and have weaker digestive acids. If you find a pellet with bones, it most likely came from an owl.

Be careful of startling birds! Some like vultures use projectile vomit as a defense mechanism. If a bunch of vultures are feeding on a carcass and get startled by a coyote, nothing is more distracting than a wad of vomit to the face. Also it's a good way to drop a lot of weight quickly to make a getaway flight faster.

BIRD BUSTING!

Can owls turn their heads all the way around?
Not quite, thanks to extra vertebrae and a single ligament on the back of the neck, owls can turn theirs 270 degrees, much farther than humans. Most birds have more flexibility than mammals because their eyes are locked in their sockets and that is the only way they can see behind themselves.

Toes

When people refer to a bird's foot, they are actually referring to their toes. If you look at a bird's foot in comparison to a human's, they are essentially standing on their toes all day. Their ankle is about halfway up the leg.

Just as important as wings, a bird's toes are essential to survival. When not flying, they are standing on their toes. Because they are on their toes so much, they tuck up one foot while sleeping to give it rest.

The skin on the bottoms of bird toes is rough, and they need rough surfaces to evenly wear off the dead skin. One of the risks to birds in captivity is a buildup of this dead skin, leading to a painful condition called bumblefoot.

Have you ever noticed birds standing on cold metal in winter and wondered how they do it? Or how do ducks, geese, and swans handle cold feet in cold water? The bird foot is made up of bone and tendons and covered by scaly skin. There are fewer nerves and blood vessels to be affected and they do not feel cold in the same way a human would. They will tuck up a foot into their feathers if it's too cold or on some occasions, tuck both feet up against their bodies. Cranes will do this while in flight on very cold mornings during migration.

Birds' feet are mostly bone and tendons, so unlike mammals, they have a limited supply of nerves, blood vessels, or muscles to freeze. And their feet are covered with scales, which aren't living tissues and are less susceptible to freezing.

Imagine if the only way you could eat your breakfast, lunch, and dinner was to grab and kill small animals with your toes. That's what raptors like eagles, hawks, owls, and falcons do. They use their sharp claws also known as talons to grab and kill their food. This is what separates these birds of prey from other meat eaters like herons, who use their beaks to grab and kill their food.

The toes of different types of raptors have varying degrees of thickness. For example, buteos like red-tailed hawks are thick since they tend to grab rabbits, squirrels, and gophers. Accipiters like sharp-shinned hawks have skinny toes since they eat mostly small, light-weight and easily crushable small songbirds.

Raptors' toes are also of different lengths. Peregrine falcons have longer toes and they tend to go for fatter birds for prey. If you are flying away with dead teal or pigeons, you need long toes to hold on to that robust breast.

Some raptors are booted, meaning their feathers go down to their toes. Golden eagle feathers go down the foot to just above the toes and most species of owls have feathers that go all the way down to the talon. This is thought to be extra protection against the elements as these birds would be diving for prey in snow and shrubbery. Snowy owls have such long toe feathers that some look like they are channeling Elvis Presley in a leisure suit with bellbottoms.

Owls and osprey have one toe that can switch places. Most birds have three toes in front and one toe in back. Owls and osprey can move one of their toes and sometimes have two in front and two in back. This helps the osprey hold on to slippery fish and aids owls when grabbing prey in low-light conditions.

Most woodpeckers have two toes in front and two toes in back to aid their ability to climb.

The American three-toed woodpecker, Eurasian three-toed woodpecker, and black-backed woodpecker only have three toes in front and no back toe. They are not as strong at climbing as other species, but studies suggest they have a harder blow when they peck.

Sanderlings have no back toe.

Ducks, geese, and swans have webbed feet that allow them to swim. Other birds do too including cormorants, pelicans, gulls, and terns.

People see coots floating around in the water and assume they are some type of duck. Though they can swim, their toes are actually lobed instead of webbed; it still affords them some paddling ability but also enables them to stand on silty ground without sinking. They will use those toes to churn up soil underwater to get at vegetation and invertebrates.

Grebes are another example of swimming birds that do not have webbed toes. They are lobed instead.

Some birds like the northern jacana have long toes. Comically long, these help them walk on floating vegetation. Though not quite as long as jacana toes, herons and egrets have long toes to enable them to stand in silty areas without sinking.

Unlike other birds, hummingbirds cannot walk on their toes. If a hummingbird is perched on a branch and wants to turn around, it must first fly up and turn around and then reperch. Swifts are the same way; they are unable to walk on their toes.

A raptor known as the gymnogene is double-jointed and uses this ability to stick its foot into tiny crevices and cavities to get at lizards, baby birds, and snakes.

Feathers

Feathers have several functions: camouflage, temperature regulation, and aiding in flight and communication.

Seriously, there is a bird hidden in this photo. It's a member of the nightjar family called a common pauraque. Their brown and gray feathers blend well with branches and leaves. High five if you can make out the bird!

One of the reasons birds can handle cold weather is that their feathers act as a great insulator. Feathers can trap heat next to the bare skin underneath, so essentially birds are always wearing a coat.

Feathers are a means of communication. Birds with crests can raise and lower them communicating how they feel about others of their species. An obvious example would be the male peacock. During breeding season, the males have long tail feathers that they raise to get the attention of females.

Feathers can also be an excellent defense. Owls are not as fast as hawks and are active at night. During the day, they use their cryptic plumage to blend in and hide from rivals. Large owls will perch next to tree trunks, blending in with the bark. Potoos take camouflage to a new level by stretching out to look exactly like a broken branch.

Feathers can also assist with speed. Falcon wing feathers are stiffer than hawk feathers. Peregrine falcon feathers are especially stiff and when they form their teardrop shape to dive, the stiff feathers aid in their ability to speed up and catch prey.

Owls are the Sunday drivers of the bird world, their wing feathers are incredibly soft and there are tiny bristles on the wing feathers. This breaks up air when they flap and makes them almost completely silent in their flight. Studies suggest that predators that hunt by stealth rather than speed tend to be more successful in grabbing prey.

Bird feathers are not always the color that they seem. Birds that are red have red pigment in the feathers, meaning if you found a red cardinal feather and ground it up, you would have red powder. Birds that appear blue do not have blue pigment in their feathers; rather their feathers are black and the shape makes them reflect the color blue. It's one of the reasons an indigo bunting can look black when lurking in the bushes.

Feathers can even help with a bird's ability to hear. If you look at the shape of an owl's face or a harrier's face, their eyes face front. All the feathers on the face are very short and sensitive to vibrations. The feathers actually guide sounds to the ears, helping them to pinpoint exactly where prey is hiding in low-light conditions.

White feathers are the weakest and tend to wear out the fastest.

Birds will go through what is called a "fright molt," meaning if they are grabbed and frightened, feathers will come loose. This is handy for smaller birds with long tails. If a predator grabs the feathers and not the body, the small bird can fly away, leaving the hawk nothing but talons full of feathers. This will affect their ability to fly well, but if they can find food and shelter while new feathers grow in, they can live to breed another day.

Can you see the western screech owl hiding in this photo?

There's an ancient falconry technique called "imping" that wildlife rehabilitators use to this day. Birds of prey come into clinics with varying degrees of injury. If a hawk's injuries are minor, but is missing wing or tail feathers, veterinarians can implant feathers from a hawk species that is already dead so the bird doesn't have to wait for a molt to bring in new feathers.

You can get an idea of a bird's flight based on its wing shape. Falcons are fast and have pointed tips to their wings; hawks have rounded wings and though they are fast, they do not come close to falcons.

The whistling swan is the current record holder for the most number of feathers at 25,216.

The ruby-throated hummingbird is thought to have the fewest feathers at 940, but we can't be sure because no one has counted the feathers of the world's smallest humming-bird, the bee hummingbird.

Most flighted birds have pores or air sacs in their bones to make them lighter in weight. In fact, the skeleton of a bald eagle weighs less than every single feather on its body combined.

Birds can look bizarre and trippy like this spoonbill, but from feathers for flight and temperature regulation to a bill perfect for swiping the ground under shallow water for food, they are perfectly designed.

Feather Maintenance

Feathers require cleaning and refurbishing, a lot like our hair does. True, birds molt out old feathers on a regular basis, and if a feather is pulled out by a predator, a new feather will start to grow, but birds must keep them in top shape.

This bobolink preens his feathers with his beak to keep his feathers in top condition.

Birds preen their feathers on a daily basis. This involves going over each feather and making sure it is in place with their beak. Think of a bird beak as a sort of hairbrush, zipping feathers back together and in place.

Much the same way humans need conditioner to prevent split ends, birds need it for their feathers too, they just happen to carry it around with them at all times in the form of a preen gland. The gland is on their back, right above the tail, and they can squeeze a bit out and rub it on their feathers with their beak as they are preening. This is what keeps duck feathers fairly waterproof. Since birds cannot preen the feathers on their head as easily, you will notice them rubbing their faces on their lower back, getting the preen gland oil on their facial feathers.

Bathing in water is an important part of feather maintenance but not all birds are content with water. Many will use dust or sand and move around and splash in it just as if it were water.

Have you ever noticed a bird on the ground with its wings and tail fanned out? You may even notice ants crawling all over their bodies. This is known as "anting" and we do not know the exact reason they do it. The common speculation is that birds allow the ants all over their feathers and body in an attempt to get rid of parasites; however it's an area that needs further study.

Ever noticed large birds like anhingas, vultures, or cormorants perched with their wings out? This is called "sunning." There are two common theories about what the birds are doing. One is an attempt to rid feathers of parasites, but the other is that it is a means of drying feathers out, or in the case of soaring birds like vultures; it warms the feathers and puts them back in shape. Again, this is an area that needs further study.

BIRD BUSTING!

Can a pelican's beak hold more than its belly can?

That is what the poet Ogden Nash proposed. And yes they can, but they don't swallow the entire contents. Different species of pelicans grab food in different ways. Some, like the brown pelican, do spectacular dives into schools of fish. Others work as a group to herd schools together while they float on the water and scoop them up. They grab a beak-full and then squeeze out the water and swallow the remaining contents—fish. Pelicans can't swallow the fish along with the water.

Eyesight

Birds have an extra eyelid called a nictitating membrane that they can see through partially. It covers their eyes when they are flying and prevents pieces of food from hitting their eyes while eating.

Birds have incredible eyesight and see the world very differently than we do. Because birds have four different color receptors, they can see in the ultraviolet spectrum. Though a male and female starling may look the same to our eyes, they can look very different to each other.

When certain flowers are viewed under ultraviolet light, it looks as though petals on nectar-rich flowers have runways guiding them in. In a garden with lots of hummingbird-friendly plants, it must almost look like the Las Vegas strip.

Kestrels are known for their ability to hover. What most people do not realize is that with their ability to see in the ultraviolet spectrum, they can see fresh mouse urine. Where there is fresh urine, there is a fresh mouse. You could safely say to your friends while observing a hovering kestrel, "Hey, that bird sees mouse pee." I cannot guarantee they will be impressed.

Bird eyes are very large in relation to their heads. In fact, owl eyes are so large in comparison to the rest of their face, that if human eyes were as large, our eyes would be about the size of softballs.

Most birds of prey have eyes so large that they are literally locked in the sockets. Owl eyes are more tubular shaped than round. Since they are unable to move their eyes from side to side the way people can, they have very flexible necks and can turn their heads 270 degrees. Most birds are able to turn their heads halfway around, but not quite as far as owls.

Birds have an extra eyelid called a nictitating membrane, as seen on this red-tailed hawk's eyes, that they can use to protect their eyes while flying in rain.

Most birds of prey have the ability to see in low-light conditions. They have more rods or light receptors in their eyes than humans. Owls have fewer cones or color receptors than hawks and eagles, but have far more rods, which allows them to see in the dark better than hawks and eagles.

Though owl eyesight is incredible, they are farsighted. They cannot see a few inches in front of their face. If you ever see an owl being fed in captivity and it is on the trainer's gloved hand, if the food is placed on the glove, they will feel around for it with their beak since they cannot see exactly where it is. When they are diving for prey, right before they land, they will place their talons directly in front of their eyes to make sure they grab it.

Woodcock eyes are set in a fashion that they are able to constantly have a 360-degree field of view.

In some species, iris color changes as the bird ages. Bird banders can use this as a tool to judge how old a bird is that they are banding. It is not an exact science, and it is not well understood. Some examples include crows that start with blue eyes; young sharp-shinned hawks start with yellow eyes and they get darker red as they get older. It's the opposite for sparrow hawks—their eyes start red and then get more yellow as they get older. Bald eagle eyes start brown and get yellow as they grow into adulthood.

Imagine that you not only have the ability to fly but also to see 360 degrees while doing so, like this woodcock.

Hearing

Bird ears are placed on the sides of their heads and are usually blocked by feathers. Birds that have tufts use those for communication and camouflage, not hearing.

Owl ears are uneven slits on either side of their heads and it is believed that the asymmetrical placement helps owls triangulate where prey is hiding under leaves and under snow.

Owl hearing is so sensitive that some species are able to hear small mammals moving under three feet of snow.

When bird calls are slowed down to one-third speed, they sound completely different. It is believed, especially in the cases of birds that can harmonize with themselves, that they hear sound in different ways than we do, and the nuance is lost on human hearing.

When large birds are young, they have no feathers covering their ears. Some flies will lay their eggs inside the large ear canals. When young eagles (see photo) and owls are brought in to wildlife rehabilitation centers, they almost always have an earful of maggots. The flies do little damage, other than muffle hearing before they pupate and fly away.

Smell

The avian sense of smell is not fully understood. It was originally thought that most birds have a poorly developed sense of smell, but as we study more, we learn that quite a few birds can smell very well.

Turkey vultures are one of the few birds with a highly developed sense of smell. Studies suggest that they can smell something dead from anywhere from one to five miles away. Turkey vultures will circle over an area with a ripe smell and are so reliable that gas pipeline workers will use them as an indicator of a leak.

Leach's storm petrels' main source of food is krill and they fly over the ocean and find it based on the aroma the krill emits. Albatrosses also have a keen sense of smell that they use to find fish over a vast expanse of ocean.

Experiments on Leach's storm petrels indicate that they use aromas to locate their burrows in the dark.

Fulmars, albatrosses (like the mollymawk in the photo), and storm petrels have tube-shaped noses that aid in removing excess salt from their bodies. This is a handy function for birds that spend most of their time over open-ocean and nowhere near fresh water.

Godwit Days

Would you believe it, there is a bird festival dedicated to the marbled godwit, a larger shorebird with a long, slightly upturned bill. The festival happens in mid-April at Arcata Marsh and Wildlife Sanctuary in California at a wastewater treatment facility, and godwits descend by the thousands to fuel up before heading to their breeding grounds. If you enjoy a bird that is obvious and easy to see and a vacation that comes with a great story like, "So we were biking through a wastewater treatment facility . . . ," then this is just what you need.

Costa Rica

Costa Rica is one of the most popular destinations for bird lovers around the world. you get a lot of bird bang for your buck, and they are crazy colorful and unique. From toucans of all sizes and shiny green quetzals with unfathomably long tails, you will be wowed. The warm temperatures and the North American birds that spend the winter here make it a paradise for those who live in snowy locations.

collared aracari toucan

CHAPTER 4

Common Questions

Once people realize you have an interest in birds, three things will begin to happen. One, people will ask to you identify birds, often with odd descriptions that defy any field guide. Two, they will give you any and all form of insane bird knickknacks, because you are, you know, "into birds." And three, you will have to explain any bird behavior they happen to notice. These are some of the most common behaviors you should be prepared to answer. And as for the bird knickknacks, all I can advise is to practice a gracious thank-you face and brace yourself for some atrocious garage sale rejects.

WHY ARE THOSE CROWS ATTACKING THAT OWL?

A very common behavior people notice is when several smaller species gang up on a larger bird, usually a predator. This is known as "mobbing." Crows do this in a loud and spectacular way when they find an owl or hawk. Aerial predators will use an element of surprise and if crows happen to notice them perched, they will caw to their other cronies and soon an entire flock is surrounding the predator, which often looks as though it would like to melt into the tree and not be noticed at all. You will even see some crows actually dive at the predatory bird. Crows have learned this is a relatively safe tactic that usually does not result in injury, but every now and then, a raptor has a lucky day.

BIRD BUSTING!

Is rebirth of an eagle real?
There's a PowerPoint presentation making the rounds on the Internet describing how eagles in their forties must fly to a mountaintop and stay there for several months to pluck out their talons, beak, and feathers and wait it out while they grow new ones. This is absolutely untrue. An eagle that has no talons or feathers and doesn't eat for five months is a dead eagle. You may think that no one will fall for it, but yes, someone will e-mail this to you or describe it and ask if it's possible.

WHY ARE THOSE SMALLER BIRDS ATTACKING THAT HAWK?

This behavior is not limited to crows. Many species do it. Even small chickadees and tits will mob a small owl. If you are ever walking in the woods and you hear something that sounds like a bunch of angry chickadees near a bush, take a moment and look closer. Often times you will find a tiny screech owl or saw-whet owl hidden inside the bush.

As you go out in the field, you will notice that several species have a specific call that they give when an aerial predator has been spotted. Both red-winged blackbirds and robins give a distinct high-pitch whistle when a Cooper's hawk or sharp-shinned hawk has been seen. Other species know this too, and if you ever hear it, look up—chances are very good you will see a small hawk fly over.

This is another form of mobbing, usually performed by blackbirds. Red-winged blackbirds can be particularly aggressive to hawks and herons, both of whom are capable of plucking chicks from nests. Red-wing males will get behind a heron or hawk and dive as the predator flies away. In rare cases, they will momentarily land on the back of the predator's neck and continue to peck, looking as though they are getting a free ride.

WHY ARE BIRDS ATTACKING MY WINDOWS?

We love to watch the birds from our windows, yet those very things are a huge contributing factor to their decline. Until we can manufacture windows that are visible to birds and their ability to see in the ultraviolet spectrum, it will continue to be a problem.

Some birds will flutter up against windows for several hours at a time. This is most common during the breeding season when a male will encounter his reflection and in many cases, fight it, mistaking it as a rival for territory. When this begins, it's incredibly hard to stop. Once the male is in the habit of looking for the rival, he will return day after day to fight it. No one solution can fix this and people try everything from Mylar tape to falcon silhouettes and wind chimes. The solution that works the best is to try and block the reflection on the outside by placing a sheet or newspaper over the window for a week to ten days, breaking the bird of the habit. Some people have reported mixed results of rubbing soap on the outside of the window as a means of blocking the reflection. Keep in mind that the soap disappears when it rains.

This American robin is fighting what he thinks is a rival but it's really his reflection that he sees in this van's windows and rearview mirrors.

Many birds will fly into windows during migration or in an effort to evade predators, or simply while trying to fly from point A to B in a backyard. The reflection from the sun makes it appear to be a safe area to fly through and instead the birds slam into a hard surface.

Some species of hawk in the accipiter family like the Cooper's hawk will drive birds into windows in an attempt to stun them. After all, it's easier to grab and eat something that is stunned or already dead than a live bird. Unfortunately for young hawks learning to hunt, they sometimes crash into the glass as well.

There are several options from window decals to netting, but the bottom line is that there is not an easy answer to stop birds from hitting windows; it will take more than one small falcon silhouette to be truly effective.

Window Decals. These need to be placed on the glass outside, not inside. Some people have luck with small falcon-shaped decals, but not because the falcon shape is scaring the bird away. It takes several decals, but they break up what could look like a clear passage to birds. Some decals are specially made to be visible in the ultraviolet spectrum and be an even brighter beacon to birds.

String, Ribbons, Mylar Tape. This is most effective if the strings or ribbons are stretched in front of the glass and held down on either end. The lines should be no more than four inches apart to be truly effective.

Ultraviolet-Patterned Glass. Some companies like Ornilux are developing glass that has patterns inside that are visible to birds in the ultraviolet spectrum, but replacing old windows with this new style of glass may be cost prohibitive.

Feeder Placement. If you have bird feeders in your yard, consider moving them closer to the windows or even attaching feeders with suction cups to the window. If birds are coming from the feeder, they will not have time to gain speed and hit the windows as hard.

Blinds. Some recommend closing the blinds or setting houseplants in front of the window. That can stop a few birds, but not all of them.

Netting. Fruit netting is available in many home and garden stores. The trick is to mount it so the netting is taut. If it's loose, birds could get tangled in it. It is also key to mount it so the nesting is two inches away from the glass so birds can bounce off of it safely. You can still see the birds out the window, but it won't be deadly.

BIRD BUSTING!

If I close my blinds, will that stop birds from hitting my windows?
Some people think that closing blinds or curtains on a window will prevent a bird from seeing its reflection and fighting it. This is not a solution. If anything, the blinds make it easier for the bird to see its reflection.

Woodpeckers need dead trees and they like the older wood because in can be chock-full of tasty insect larvae and it works well for creating nest holes. And since woodpeckers are not known for their ability to sing a beautiful song, males will drum on resonant trunks and branches to attract a female. As people cut down dead and dying trees, woodpeckers improvise and find houses covered in cedar siding as an acceptable substitute and will peck on those.

If a bird such as a hairy woodpecker has set its sites on your home, you want to take immediate action. Once woodpeckers get the chance to make one hole, it gets increasingly difficult to dissuade them.

In some cases, woodpeckers can be attracted to insects like leafcutter bees that lay eggs in the gaps in cedar siding. In others, they can be attracted to stovepipe chimneys or gutters because they carry the sound of their drumming far and wide to get a female's attention.

If it's a case of acorn woodpeckers, you must act swiftly. This species lives in family groups, and they are famous for their ability to create storage. Typically, in the wild, the family group would select a large tree and store thousands upon thousands of acorns in it. They peck a small hole and wedge the acorn into it. As urban housing sprawls, more and more acorn woodpeckers select homes with cedar siding.

Once this activity starts, it's imperative that you try to nip it in the bud. The longer a woodpecker is able to peck on your home, the harder it is to deter. Once a woodpecker has made a few holes in the side of a home, it can serve as a beacon to woodpeckers passing through that someone may have found food there and encourage them to come down and peck some more. If the holes are large and deep enough, they can get the attention of starlings and kestrels looking for a nesting cavity.

BIRD BUSTING!

Birdmaggedon?

While ringing in the New Year for 2011, several residents in the small town of Beebe, Arkansas, woke to find thousands of birds falling from the sky. The blackbirds and grackles were dead on impact, but a few were found with wing injuries on the ground. Soon, people were compiling maps of mass animal die-offs and worried the dead birds were a sign of the end times or at least an alien invasion.

Investigators determined that the birds died after being startled by a New Year's fireworks display. The species involved do not see well in the dark and flew into each other, into homes, trees, or right into the ground after being startled awake.

Some scoffed that birds don't die in large flocks during typical celebrations in the summer, but the time of year made all the difference. In the winter, many species of blackbirds including grackles, red-winged blackbirds, and cowbirds form huge winter roosts, numbering in the tens of thousands. These birds roost in trees and if something startles a large flock like that, quite a few deaths will happen. In the summer during fireworks celebrations, birds are not in large winter roosts; they are at their own nests tending young. They are startled and certainly some birds (and bats) are killed, but not to the scale of setting off a mortar next to trees filled with thousands of sleeping blackbirds.

SOLUTIONS

🪶 **Replace Siding.** The best solution and most expensive is to get rid of cedar siding and go with aluminum. This option may not suit everyone's budget.

🪶 **Hang Shiny Objects.** Try discouraging the woodpeckers by hanging out shiny metallic objects like red Mylar tape. It's important that the items be hung over the area the woodpeckers are attacking and that they are attached by string, so they can sway in the breeze. The movement and the shininess is what is supposed to deter them.

🪶 **Motion Detectors.** A recent and popular solution has been motion sensitive detectors. There's one that started as a popular Halloween decoration but works well for woodpecker tactics. When the device senses motion, a large, hairy spider drops down on a cord and bounces around. After a few moments, the spider retreats into the device. Since it works every time it senses movement, it does a good job of freaking the woodpeckers out.

That red-bellied woodpecker eyeing your house isn't purposely trying to drive you insane. It is simply using your home like a dying tree. Once woodpeckers make a hole on your house, it's imperative that you act fast to deter them.

WHY IS THAT BIRD ATTACKING ME?

In general, birds want to stay as far away from humans as possible. We're big and unpredictable, and for most species, we are considered a predator. But sometimes birds fly at our heads. This mostly happens during nesting season, especially right before the young leave the nest. Adults like to put on a good show so the young birds realize some of the dangers they face in the wild.

Birds that dive at heads tend to get more brazen. They may have started diving at people's heads along a park path and a jogger with headphones may be oblivious to the swooping bird behind them. In the hawk's mind, it has learned that diving made this person go away even if that person was just walking a path. The hawk may try getting closer to get the people in its territory to move away faster, and it may eventually make contact with a scalp. Once the chicks leave the nest, the behavior will stop. It's incredibly rare for it to happen but if it does, there's an age-old solution. Duck. Also, consider wearing a hat.

The other reason a bird may fly at your head is that it has been imprinted on humans. Well-intentioned people will sometimes illegally raise a baby bird to adulthood and release it. If an untrained person does this, the baby bird can imprint on humans, associating them with food or in a worse-case scenario, think of people as a potential mate.

If it is not nesting season and a bird is diving at your head, call your local animal control or wildlife rehabilitator. An imprinted bird is a danger to itself and to others.

BIRD BUSTING!

If you have a problem with birds, a fake plastic owl will solve the problem.
Fake owls are a waste of money. They may keep birds away for a few days, but once the birds notice that the owl never moves, they simply ignore it. There have even been cases of birds building nests on owl statues. In some instances, they may even attract noisy birds. There's a video on the Internet of a Cooper's hawk diving at an owl statue for several minutes while screaming loudly at it.

Crows form roosts of thousands of birds in the winter.

Starlings form large flocks called "murmurations" in the winter. Even though these birds are "common," and in some countries a nuisance, watching a murmuration maneuver to evade predators rivals any performance you'll find in New York or London's West End.

When mating season is over, some species will sleep in huge communal roosts. These large flocks settling in for the night can offer a spectacular display. European starlings, blackbirds, purple martins, and chimney swifts all put on incredible flight displays. Blackbirds and starlings, in particular, will practically form artistic shapes in the sky as they settle down.

Being part of a large flock has one huge advantage. If you are one of ten thousand, you are less likely to be eaten by a hawk or an owl. One would think that a peregrine falcon would have no trouble nailing one starling in a huge flock, but the way the flock moves makes it difficult for the fast-flying falcon to focus on just one bird.

Even crows and rooks will form huge roosts in the winter as they settle in to sleep at night. Many of these roosts are shifting locations from remote wooded areas to inner cities.

Part of the reason is urban sprawl, but the other reason is that crows are less likely to be shot at and disturbed in an urban park than on some farmer's back lot.

If a blackbird or crow roost is in your area, watch it one night at dusk. The immense size of the flock descending on the trees is something everyone should witness at least once in their life. It is spectacular.

Many species of birds form large winter roosts and sleep together at night. Being one of thousands decreases your chances of being eaten by a predator. There's more than one species of blackbird in this flock. How many can you identify? Pro Tip: the large white bird is a snow goose not a blackbird.

Tool Use

A few bird species have turned the scientific world on its ear with their demonstration of intelligence and tool use. Two have even demonstrated the ability to create a tool, something that only mammals were known to do. Scientists enjoy a good argument for what exactly constitutes tool use, but if you define it as an animal using an object that is not part of their own body to accomplish a task, then you will notice a few tool users in the bird world.

🪶 Green herons and striated herons have been observed using bait to catch fish by dropping leaves, bread, or seeds that float on top of the water to attract small fish.

🪶 On the Galápagos Islands resides the woodpecker finch, known in textbooks around the world as one of the few birds that not only uses tools, but creates them as well. The finches take a twig, stick, or cactus spine and manipulate it to get grubs from trees, sometimes using their beaks to adjust the length for easier use. Some studies show that these birds acquire up to 50 percent of their prey using tools during the dry season.

🪶 New Caledonian crows shocked the scientific community by not only using tools, but a female of the species took a wire and formed it into a hook to get access to food. The birds have also been observed teaching toolmaking to their young.

🪶 One could argue that the satin bowerbird is a tool user since the male uses plant fibers as a paintbrush to coat mashed fruit and saliva on his bower to attract a female. The bower looks like a little shelter made of vegetation, but it's not used for nesting; it's strictly for getting a female's attention.

🪶 Lammergeiers, also known as bearded vultures, will carry animal bones high into the air and drop them many times on sharp rocks to crack open and splinter off pieces of bone to gain access to their preferred food, bone marrow.

Several species of gulls will drop clams onto hard pavement or rocks to crack open the hard shells to get to the nourishing slime inside.

Carrion crows in Japan have been observed setting nuts at traffic intersections. The birds wait for traffic to stop, set down the nuts, and fly up to a perch to wait for a car to run over the nut so it can access the meat.

Barn swallows in Minneapolis figured out how to activate the motion sensor to the doors of a Home Depot. The birds built their nest inside the store and would either fly through when customers passed into the store, or fly in front of the sensor, triggering the doors to open. Many birds learn by trial and error. The birds probably figured out that when they flew to a certain spot, the doors would open. It's a clever strategy to keep predators from discovering the nest!

Cooperative Hunting

Most birds prefer to hunt for food on their own unless they are in a flock that is descending on a pile of seeds. Generally, birds don't work together to get food. But a few do.

Harris's hawks are so well known for their ability to hunt in a pack, that falconers enjoy using them for group hunts. In the wild, groups of two to six birds will coordinate efforts to flush, direct, and attack large prey.

Lanner falcon pairs will cooperatively hunt, and each member of the pair will have distinct roles. Males tend to steer prey toward the larger female to kill, though she does not always share in the reward.

A classy looking hawk, this raptor ups its cool factor by hunting in a group to get prey like jack rabbits.

Aberrant and Deformed Birds

Eventually as you watch birds, you'll notice something that seems a little off. A bird may have patches of white, may be the wrong color, or be much darker. It could be a case of a genetic mutation or it may even be the result of forbidden love.

A flash of white passes by your window, so you go to look and find a flock of sparrows and one is completely white. It may get picked on by the other sparrows but apart from being white, the bird is shaped like a sparrow. If the bird has pink legs, beak, and eyes, it is an albino and completely lacks pigment in any of its feathers.

Perhaps you noticed a flash of black and white mixed in with some blackbirds. There's a bird among them that is the same shape, is mostly black, but has a few chunks of white in its feathers. The common assumption is that it is a partial albino. This drives scientists crazy; technically albinism is an all-or-nothing thing—you can't go halfway.

Perhaps you see a catbird, but it's not dark. You can see the basic plumage, but it's kind of faded out. This can also be referred to as leucism.

The bird in your backyard looks like a northern cardinal. It's all red; however the head is tiny and black. This is a bald cardinal. This condition has also been observed in blue jays, screech owls, and grackles. There are currently two different theories, but not a lot of agreement. It seems to be observed in late summer and early fall.

One theory is that the birds have feather mites. Normally a bird can use their beaks to clean and maintain their feathers but they would not be able to get at the feathers on their heads and the mites chew all the feathers down. By the time the birds grow in new feathers, it's winter and the cold weather will have killed off the mites.

Another theory is that for certain individuals in the population, this is a normal occurrence. When they molt or grow in new feathers, all the feathers on their head fall at the same time. One thing is certain; it's an area that needs further study.

Sometimes you get birds that are the wrong color. In Ohio and Kentucky, there have been cardinals that are yellow when they should be red. It's a strange genetic mutation and a good example of how you never know what will be in your yard.

House finch males are typically a bright pink, but the shade of pink depends on their diet. They need carotenoids and males with the brighter pink plumage communicate to females that they have access to a lot of them and that's a good territory. Males that are yellow or orange communicate to females that they have a lesser territory.

BIRD BUSTING!

Do crows go sledding?

There's a video of a hooded crow that looks like it's riding a tiny inner tube down a snow-covered roof. People love to forward it in e-mails and proclaim that the crow is sledding for fun.

There is no doubt the crow is sliding down a roof on a round structure. But if you watch the behavior, the crow is pecking at something round, possibly a doughnut or lid with some food on it. Crows like to eat their food on a high perch so no ground predators will steal it. This crow has chosen a peaked roof, and every time it tries to peck at the food, it slides down the side of the roof. This bird can't seem to figure out that a round structure on a peaked roof is going to lead to an Olympic sport.

Some researchers argue that corvids like crows and ravens exhibit behaviors that are clearly play. However, others insist that no animal is capable of such behavior. If you bring this topic up around scientists, tread carefully and be prepared for rolling eyes and an argument.

Vacation Idea

Central Park, New York City, New York

Believe it or not, some of the best bird-watching can happen right in New York City. Green space with a habitat for birds to find food, water, and shelter is at a premium in urban areas and Central Park is a prime example of that. When planning a trip to the Big Apple, you can take in museums, a Broadway show, and fabulous food, and still have time for a stroll through the park and find the famous red-tailed hawks like Pale Male, as well as owls, herons, and every variety of warbler. Guided bird walks are also offered, so you if you prefer to go birding in a group or are new, you can find some companions. This area is so popular, a documentary about it called *The Central Park Effect* was released in 2012.

Crow Roost in the U.S.

If you would like a fun winter evening activity that will knock your socks off, look for a crow roost. They are all over the U.S. from November through the end of February. To find a roost near you, carefully follow lines of crows in your car at dusk or visit www.crowsnet/roost-lst.html.

Somerset Levels and Moors, Somerset, England

Starling murmations can be found all over, but one of the most epic ones is found from November through February at Westhay Moor and Shapwick Heath. Fill a thermos full of cocoa (or take a flask of whiskey if you're not driving) and enjoy the show. Even the most curmudgeonly anti-bird person will be in awe.

CHAPTER 5

Migration

Most swallows only eat insects and must time their migration carefully. Tree swallows will eat berries if insects are not available, making it possible for them to arrive earlier and leave later than other species of swallow.

When you think about migration, you begin to wonder what it is exactly to be a resident bird. Most people tend to think of a bird as a resident when they build a nest and raise chicks. However, for some bird species, like the common nighthawk, the birds spend more days of the year on their wintering grounds in South America, rather than the breeding grounds. Wouldn't that then make them a visitor on their nesting grounds rather than a resident? Fortunately, birds don't hold elections or pay taxes, so it's not that big of a deal to them if you think they are a resident by nesting in your yard.

Migration appears to be a response to food supply. Some birds that winter in the tropics and need to raise young have evolved to journey to the north where there would be ample food and less competition. Birds that do not migrate and spend their lives in the north do not face the dangers, uncertainties like storms, or lack of food along the way like in the south. However, they risk the cold, snow, and limited food of winter. It's a gamble either way.

For species that migrate, their bodies will shift and hormone levels tell them to eat as much as possible and increase their body weight. Researchers who study birds by placing bands on their legs will blow onto the breast feathers of birds. The skin is translucent and you can see how much fat has accumulated. They can predict based on fat and wind forecast when that bird would leave.

How Far Will Birds Go?

The short answer is as far as they have to go to find food, water, and shelter. For some species, that might be going from southern Canada into the northern United States and for other species it might mean going from the Tundra all the way down to Brazil.

The bird with the longest nonstop flight is the bar-tailed godwit. It will fly about 6,300 miles. One satellite-tagged bird flew a total of 6,851 over a period of nine days without stopping from New Zealand to the Yellow Sea in China.

Arctic terns get the medal for the longest journey for migration as they travel between the North Pole and the South Pole. The shortest journey documented was 36,900 miles but the average distance is roughly 44,000 miles.

Birds that soar for most of their migration like hawks, pelicans, storks, eagles, and vultures migrate during the day. They need thermals, warm currents of air that rise in a circular fashion, to lift them up as they glide south. Soaring allows them to spend less energy and being larger birds, they are safe flying in the middle of the day.

Twice a year, the rufous hummingbird travels 3,000 miles between its breeding grounds in Alaska and its wintering grounds in Mexico.

The bar-headed goose is believed to be the highest-flying migrant. They have been reported flying over 27,800 feet over Mount Makalu, and there's even an unconfirmed report of them flying over Mount Everest at just over 29,000 feet.

Small passerines like this blue-winged warbler migrate at night in an effort to avoid migrating hawks.

Birds that do not soar and flap continuously tend to migrate at night, using the stars as a guide. Most of these birds are small and would be prey for hawks and falcons. Flying at night gives them a bit of safety from predators. However, there are new dangers, since these birds can get easily distracted by lights on buildings, cell towers, and wind turbines.

Some birders will watch wind forecasts and on nights with favorable winds, stay up and listen for the chips of thousands of migrating birds flying overhead. To the human ear, most of these chip notes sound the same, but when you look at the sonograms of the chip note, each species is unique. Some birders will record these sounds and use a sonogram to identify what was flying overhead.

Individuals in a species may choose to not migrate. Peregrine falcons are a mixed bag, some head south and others stick out the winter. This can lead to awkward situations with mated pairs if the female migrates, leaving the male behind. In her absence, he may pair up with another female who did not migrate, leading to a violent, and sometimes lethal reunion when the migratory female returns.

🪶 Many American kestrel males do not migrate, while the females do. One theory is that the female is larger and needs more prey on a day-to-day basis than the male. She heads south to warmer areas and a wider prey base, while the smaller male stays and can survive on limited prey availability.

🪶 Some birds migrate up and down a mountain. This is called altitudinal migration. They may stay in the same country all year, but as storms worsen in winter, they shift to a lower elevation until the weather improves.

🪶 One of the really incredible things about migration is that during peak periods in the spring and fall, there can be so many birds in the air at night that the flocks are detectable by radar. When the phenomena was first noticed, no one knew what was causing the splotches on radar at night when skies were clear in the spring and fall. They were called phantom echoes. Now that we know more about bird movement, many birders like to keep track of regional radar through NOAA during the spring and fall.

BIRD BUSTING!

You must take your hummingbird feeder in by Labor Day or hummingbirds will not migrate.
That is not true. Your hummingbird nectar is not enough of an attractant to encourage a hummingbird to forget about migration. Birds flying south from Canada will appreciate the bonus fuel after Labor Day, and there is some evidence to suggest that some hummingbirds are expanding their winter range farther north. You may end up with a surprise rufous hummingbird in your yard.

Irruptions

Periodically we have a movement of birds that is not quite a true migration. Some northern species like snowy owls and northern goshawks will push down into southern regions in the winter. Usually this is on a ten- to twelve-year basis and is based on prey availability. The food that these raptors need to eat is on a similar cycle and about every decade or so, the prey base crashes and there are more predators than prey. The older, more experienced birds will drive the young out of the territory and the young birds will fly as far south as they need to in order to find food.

Some notable irruptions have happened in last century. One was the winter of 2004–2005 when thousands of great gray owls descended on the states of Minnesota and Wisconsin. These three-foot-long owls are diurnal, or active during the day, and it was common to drive around in certain areas and find over fifty individual owls perched in the open looking for food. Another was the snowy owl irruption of 2011–2012 when the large white owls were found as far south as Dallas, Texas. One bird was reportedly found at Honolulu Airport and was shot by a USDA officer who didn't know any other way to get the owl off the tarmac.

Even though snowy owls are expected to descend into the lower latitudes during irruption years, there are always a few who will sneak down into the United States in the northern areas. They can be found reliably at airports in the

Northern hawk owls are an irruptive species. Some years, several will travel south and other years, none will.

northern states. After all, snowy owls come from the Arctic where there are no trees and young birds coming south stop when they find the first place that resembles the tundra, usually a treeless airport. The downside is that airport security tends to frown on people staring at the jet way with binoculars, spotting scopes, and cameras.

One of the downsides of irruptions is that it is mostly the young of the year who come down and by the time they are found by people, many are starving to the point when they can no longer digest solid food. It is believed that most of the predatory birds that come down in an irruption do not return north in the spring, but die on the journey from starvation or collisions with cars and unfamiliar predators.

Other irruptions that can happen are with northern finches like redpolls and siskins. These tiny birds form huge nomadic flocks that forage the land looking for catkins and tree seeds. If there is a bad crop up in the Arctic, they will push down into more southern latitudes looking for food. People who sell birdseed love these winters because you generally don't get one redpoll or siskin, you get hundreds. Winters with a finch irruption will empty a bird feeder full of five pounds of seed in half a day.

Snowy owls are another irruptive species, though most years, snowies can be found at airports in the northern United States and Canada.

HOW LONG DOES IT TAKE?

It truly does vary from species to species. It also depends on the destination and weather patterns. Some birds may only need a few weeks, while others need a few months. And while some seem to return on very specific dates, others go with the flow. For example, species that depend on water for food and safety have to wait for the ice to go out on northern lakes. Birds that rely on fish like osprey or loons will move north in spring as water opens up.

Some spring mornings, people might notice large flocks of birds flying south instead of north. This is reverse migration; birds like geese that went far north only to find iced-over water will head south to the last spot they saw open water.

Ducks like this wood duck only go as far as they need to in migration. They can take a little snow and sub-freezing temperatures so long as they can find food and an open source of water for safe roosting at night.

HOW FAST CAN BIRDS FLY?

Peregrine falcons are noted as the fastest bird on the planet—one was clocked going over 270 miles per hour in a dive! That's extreme; generally peregrines approach two hundred miles per hour in a dive, but that's not powered flight or flapping.

When it comes to powered flight, most birds can go forty to sixty miles per hour, and due to body ratio, even a hummingbird could keep up with a goose. The fastest bird, when it comes to flapping and not gliding or diving, is the spine-tailed swift at 108 miles per hour.

Woodcocks appear to be the slowest bird in flight, coming in at only six miles per hour.

Flight speed varies based on wind and traffic. Birds will want to move on days when they can get a bit of a push from favorable winds, but if a storm system is coming, they will fly in adverse conditions.

Many species that are banded are shot by hunters, and it's a dark way for researchers to find out how far birds can travel on migration in a matter of days. But thanks to these sorts of recoveries, amazing things have been documented. Based on some of these banding studies, a blue-winged teal traveled an average of 125 miles a day and a lesser yellowlegs traveled an average of 316 miles a day.

BIRD BUSTING!

Hummingbirds migrate on the backs of Canada geese.
False. Ruby-throated hummingbirds will actually fly across the Gulf of Mexico on their own two wings.

For such a tiny bird, the willow warbler can go far. Some birds travel over 7,400 miles twice a year for migration.

Migratory Hot Spots

A fun trip to plan for bird-watching is a stop to a migratory habitat. As birds head south, there are preferred routes. There are several around the world and the key is to look for places next to a large body of water like the ocean. Birds want to avoid flying over large expanses over water to conserve energy and will follow coastlines north and south.

In North America, birds of prey want to avoid flying over Lake Superior and thousands of eagles, hawks, and falcons will get funneled over the town of Duluth, Minnesota. An observatory called Hawk Ridge was established there and every day between mid-August and mid-September, naturalists and bird banders document the phenomena. It's not out of the question to have sixteen to twenty thousand hawks fly over in a day and they've even had a record day when more than one hundred thousand broad-winged hawks were sighted.

Staging areas are also amazing to watch. The Hula Valley in Israel is a huge migratory hot spot for watching Eurasian species flying south into Africa. Thousands of storks, pelicans, kites, cranes, and eagles pass through as they head south. Israel has employed a unique strategy to aid farmers from having their fields raided by cranes. Some fields are set aside for the cranes to feed in and professional bird flushers patrol the ones that are off limits. They drive into the flocks making lots of noise, even using fireworks to scare the cranes off and encouraging them to use the fields set aside for their feeding.

Common cranes stop over in the Hula Valley in northern Israel before heading further south into Africa. Though in recent years, some thirty thousand cranes have spent the winter in Israel.

Torpor

Hibernation is associated with mammals but some birds will go into a sort of hibernation called torpor—the body temperature lowers, their metabolic rate is reduced, and they are inactive. This can be observed in hummingbirds on cold nights during migration. People will notice a hummingbird at the feeder in the morning and it will not move. In rare cases, their feet lock on the perch, but they hang upside down. The bird simply needs to warm up and feed on nectar, and set right side up.

A stationary hummingbird on a cool morning may be still in a mild state of torpor. Hummingbirds like this beryelline hummingbird can lower their metabolism and temperature when it's cold to prevent their bodies from using up all their calories while sleeping on cold nights.

Common poorwills are small nightjars related to whip-poor-wills and can go into a state of torpor for several weeks, allowing them to survive when it's too cold for insects to be out. It's not a true hibernation but it's the closest that any bird comes to it. When most animals hibernate, they go underground. The poorwill's cryptic plumage allows it to stay hidden in plain site.

Human-Made Dangers

The changes humans have made to the landscape in the last two hundred years are remarkable. Birds have had landmarks and important fueling areas erased and have had to make compromises to continue on their biannual marathon between breeding grounds and wintering spots.

Skyscrapers along migratory corridors have killed millions of migrating birds. Fatal Light Awareness Program (FLAP) has started a campaign to encourage tall office buildings to have every employee shut off lights at night during migration. They research ways to combat the problem and try to educate the public. According to FLAP, a single building kills between one to ten birds a year. If you consider that a city like Toronto has over 950,000 buildings, that is a devastating number of birds killed.

Wind energy is gaining in popularity as a replacement for relying on coal. The challenge is that some of the best areas for wind turbines are in migratory corridors and can have disastrous results. A wind farm in Altima Pass in California was one of the first to go up and it has been lethal to birds of prey, especially golden eagles. Fortunately, turbine construction has changed over the years and the blades run slower. Most companies now do environmental assessments to minimize the damage of where turbines go, but we still have lots to learn.

Some suggest putting turbines in the oceans but that would harm seabird populations. One of the jobs wind farm companies have is regular checks for bird and bat carcasses after a farm is in place to get an idea of how many species and what kinds are being affected. This is challenging on land because most species migrate at night and if they hit a turbine, chances are good that a scavenger like a raccoon, fox, or coyote will eat the fallen bird before it's located. In the ocean, it would be even harder to find the remains of birds like albatrosses, petrels, terns, pelicans, and shearwaters.

Turbines can work, but birders must be vigilant and ensure their voices are heard to make sure the placement of the turbines will not be harmful to birds.

Airports are a danger to birds but also to humans when birds strike a plane. When cities were figuring out airport locations, no one suspected that placing them along migratory routes might be a costly and lethal decision.

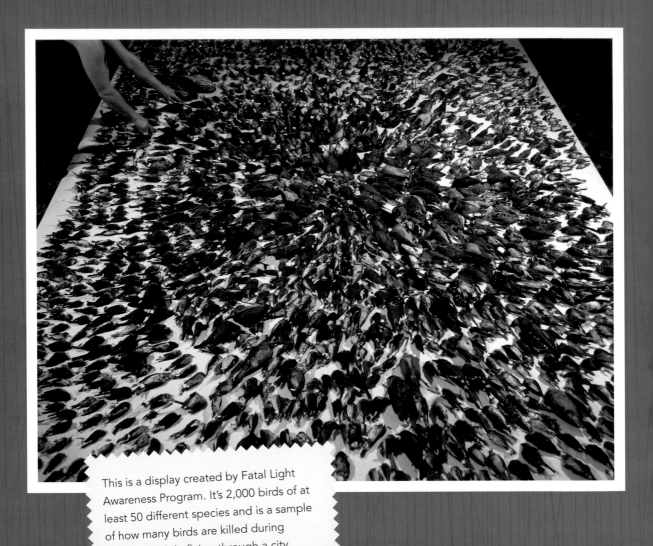

This is a display created by Fatal Light Awareness Program. It's 2,000 birds of at least 50 different species and is a sample of how many birds are killed during migration while flying through a city.

When Captain C. B. Sullenberger made his emergency landing on the Hudson River in New York, Canada geese hit the engine causing the crash. Scientists were able to get DNA samples from what little remained. Not only did they determine the species, but they also determined the birds were not from the New York area. This makes New York's decision to round up and kill resident geese puzzling. Birds that grow up around airports learn to avoid the planes and help keep intruders out.

Israel is a huge migratory corridor, and the government has the most sophisticated and very successful program for preventing migrating birds from hitting the planes. An old radar system is used to detect bird flocks. Meanwhile, watchers are placed on the ground to confirm radar sightings. Pilots also go through annual training to remind them of the best flight maneuvers and elevation when certain species are reported. So someone watching the radar would see a shape and then radio to a ground observer, "There appears to be an echo of a medium-sized flock of cranes approaching from the northwest. Can you confirm?"

The ground observer would scan the skies and say, "The radar may show cranes, but I've got a medium flock of storks in my binocular view."

"Copy that, ground observer. We will alert the pilot for safe maneuvers for flying around storks."

Bird strike fatalities have decreased almost 80 percent in Israel thanks to this amazing system. Can you imagine having a job where you not only got paid to watch birds, but your ability to identify the flock helped save lives? For many birders, that is a dream!

Another danger to migrating birds is the fact that they do not belong to one country. A bird may be protected in the United States and Canada, but it can be a different story in another country. Whimbrels are a type of shorebird that is illegal to hunt in the United States, Canada, and Mexico. In order to learn more about whimbrel migration and as a joint project with the Center for Conservation Biology at the College of William and Mary, the Nature Conservancy, the US Fish and Wildlife Service, Georgia Department of Natural Resources, the Virginia Coastal Zone Management Program, and Manomet Center for Conservation Sciences, some birds were tracked with a satellite transmitter and information about their journey was posted regularly online. A particular fan favorite was named Machi who was tracked going over twenty-seven thousand miles over the course of two years. On its last journey, the bird managed to survive flying around Hurricane Maria only to be shot as part of a legal hunt on a Caribbean island.

Many birds like this lazuli bunting are international travelers. The many small things we can do to help them can add up and make a difference.

Hunting whatever birds pass over some of the islands is a family tradition and hobby. There is no bag limit on how many birds can be shot, and many have no idea where the birds come from or what their population status is. Education about migratory birds is key and perhaps if the Caribbean islands can grow a bird-watching tourism business, it might change people's minds about changing the hunting laws.

Malta has a history of wonton trapping and shooting of wild birds. When it joined the European Union, it started an intense conflict between the bird hunters and conservationists. As members of the European Union, Malta is required to follow the Birds Directive and regulate hunting and trapping. Malta is located in the central Mediterranean flyway between Africa and Europe, and it is a resting spot for many migrating species. However, the intense hunting and trapping has not only wiped out resident birds, but has been a factor in the decline of many migratory raptors and passerines. Birders have staged camps and tours to monitor the activity and force the Maltese government to honor the EU Birds Directive.

A small shorebird called a red knot uses Delaware Bay as an area to fuel up during migration. It's estimated that 90 percent of the entire population of the red knot could be found on the bay in a single day. However, the population has plummeted since the 1980s. Some reports estimate a population decline of 90 percent since the 1980s starting at 100,000 to 51,300 in 2000; 30,000 in 2004; to just 17,200 in 2006. The problem is overharvesting of horseshoe crabs. It's popular bait for conch, whelk, and eel, but the eggs are crucial fuel for the migrating birds. If regulations on horseshoe crabs are not enacted soon, the red knot could go the way of the passenger pigeon or Carolina parakeet.

Migratory Habitat

People who love birds want to do what they can to attract them so they will nest in our yards but migratory habitat is just as important. That includes places birds stop for refueling for migration, as well as where they spend time on their wintering grounds. If everyone did one or two little things, they could significantly increase a migratory bird's chance of survival.

Drink shade-grown coffee. That's right, the coffee that so many of us consume on a daily basis—and several cups at a time—can be used to help the birds we see in our backyards. Originally, coffee was a plant grown in the shade. As the plant has been bred and mutated over the years, it became a full sun-loving plant and millions of acres of habitat have been mown down for our coffee-drinking pleasure. Birds cannot survive on coffee plants, and the farmers don't want them in there anyway. As more awareness is created, many coffee plantations are switching back to the original coffee plants and growing them in the shade. Migratory birds cannot live on coffee but they can roost in the trees that shade the coffee plants and eat insects or fruit lurking among the leaves. When purchasing coffee, always look for a shade-grown variety. Many coffee chains now offer it as an alternative.

Plant native fruit-bearing trees and shrubs. There are all sorts of varieties. Have a chat with your local nursery about what is native to your area. The food can serve a valuable purpose throughout the year. Some fruits are sweet as soon as they ripen and are readily eaten by birds in late summer and early fall. Other berries are not tasty until they have had a few months to lose moisture and are eaten by birds returning from migration in the spring.

Consult your local nursery about what plants are best for your yard. For example, birds readily eat buckthorn, but when they poop out the seeds, it spreads like crazy. It was introduced as a decorative shrub in the United States, but when left to its own devices in the

Migrating sparrow like this swamp sparrow appreciate a brush pile to roost in for safety during spring and fall migration.

wild, buckthorn will take over woods and crowd out other plants. Though birds eat buckthorn, they cannot live on that alone.

It's not just fruit-bearing trees that are great for migrating birds, you can also offer cover in the form of brush piles or conifers. Migrating birds need safe areas to rest, and a brush pile not only offers many perches for small birds but a safe haven from migrating hawks as well.

Keep your housecat indoors. Birds exhausted from migration land in yards seeking rest and food. They are easy pickings for a cat and really, how sad is it when a bird that has traveled hundreds of miles in a night—quite possibly only ninety miles away from its nesting territory—gets killed by a cat looking for something to play with?

BIRD BUSTING!

Some birds burrow underground to survive the winter.
Before we realized where some birds went in the winter, it was believed that some birds burrowed underground and slept for the winter. That is an old wives' tale.

Scott Weidensaul once wrote that some bird somewhere is migrating, even as you read that sentence. We are familiar that bird movement happens in spring and fall, but the definition of when that spring or fall movement begins to a bird is different than our timeline dictated by months listed on a calendar.

Vacation Ideas

Cape May, New Jersey

Some in Cape May might have you believe that this is where serious bird-watching got started in the United States. It is an incredible migratory hot spot, and many field guide authors in the United States cut their teeth along the shores. Though this is a popular tourist spot for beach vacationers, some of the best times to visit are during the off-season and traffic and hotel rates are not that bad. Cape May has hawk watches, seabird viewing, and crazy migratory phenomena happen like over a million American robins migrating through in a single day. Whether you visit in spring or fall, you will have a birdy time and most likely meet some of the birding elite. It hosts the most well-known birding competition: the World Series of Birding every spring.

Veracruz, Mexico

This is truly the place to be in late fall. Millions of birds migrate south from around North America and they have two choices before heading into Central and South America: either cross the Gulf of Mexico or funnel around Central America. Soaring birds lack the ability for powered flight over the Gulf so millions of birds of prey migrate over the eastern coast of Mexico and many pass over Mexico. Some tour companies have made a nice business for themselves promoting a fall hawk-watching tour. How easy and fun is it? You sit on top of a hotel sipping margaritas and watch a few million Swainson's hawks and turkey vultures pass over. It's a truly unique way to enjoy Mexico and a fun way to introduce someone who knows nothing about birds how fun, relaxed, and crazy they can be.

CHAPTER 6

Bird Love

(It's About Quantity, Not Quality)

How Birds Do It

You might be thinking that if bald eagles are that intense in the preamble, what must the actual sex act be like? Sadly, for most birds, sex is awkward and brief, yet performed several times in a row to insure fertilization. Some birds like the northern goshawk really go for the gold and may copulate as many as five hundred to six hundred times per batch of eggs!

In order to understand how birds do it, we need to look at the parts involved. It's not simply a matter of inserting tab A into slot B. A good literal description is the vernacular, "bumping uglies." Birds have different sexual organs than mammals, some surprising, some quite terrifying.

Brian Ralphs, Wikimedia Commons

The act of mating is at best awkward and brief for birds, especially those with crazy adaptations like the enormous beaks of these channel-billed toucans.

Ninety-seven percent of male bird species do not have a penis, but a cloaca, a multifaceted opening that allows birds to exit waste, urine, and sperm. Females also have a cloaca to accept sperm from males.

During the breeding season, male cloacas become swollen and enlarged. This is called a cloacal protuberance. This bird boner can last for days, even weeks. The female cloacal opening also swells during breeding season but isn't nearly as prominent as the male swelling.

They may not mate in the air, but it's still quite a feat for a male clay-colored sparrow to balance on the back of a female while she is balanced on a thin branch.

Bird mating is often referred to as the "cloacal kiss" as the male's goal is to touch his cloaca to the female's cloaca. This act lasts one to two seconds and because the sex act is so brief, birds mate as many times as possible. When it comes to sex and birds, it's not about quality, it's about quantity.

When researchers and bird banders are trying to tell males and females apart in species where both have the same coloration, they look for a swollen cloacal protuberance in males, and a bare patch on the chest and stomach on females called a brood patch. Both of these disappear after the breeding season and researchers cannot determine sex in some species, even when the bird is right in front of them.

🌿 Most birds do not mate in the air. The male must find a way to balance on top of the female. Penguins have it a bit easier as the female lies on the ground and moves her tail to the side. Other birds like eagles have to be more careful. While the female is perched on a branch, the male must climb on top and quickly commit the act.

🌿 A few bird species like waterfowl and ostriches do have penises. The most notable belongs to the male Argentine lake duck, which, on average, has a corkscrew penis that is nearly eight inches long, half the length of the bird's body. One record-breaking specimen was found in 2001 that has a penis almost seventeen inches long.

🌿 The Australian blue-billed duck is said to have such a large penis that when the male finishes copulation, he must turn on his back and stuff his penis back into the cloaca.

Richard Ashurst, Wikimedia Commons

This may be a small duck but don't underestimate what this Australian blue-billed duck is packing down below.

🌿 In duck species where the male has a long, corkscrew penis, females tend to have convoluted vaginas that are long with several pockets, some of which are dead ends. The male may force his aggressive and long penis in her, but she can choose whether or not it actually fertilizes an egg.

Greg Tee, Wikimedia Commons

The red-billed buffalo weaver has a pseudopenis, which he uses to massage against the female's genitalia, increasing the chances his sperm will stick. Unlike most other bird copulations, the buffalo weaver can go anywhere from ten to twenty seconds. That's like tantric sex with Sting in the bird world.

Anatomy gets crazy when it comes to cassowaries, as both sexes have a penis and clitoris and another genital opening that also serves as an anus. Both male and female birds have a phallus, but it is not connected to reproductive tissues in either bird. When the male cassowary inserts what looks like a penis, the semen ejaculates from the cloaca at the base. With cassowaries, anything goes.

In most species, males are more brightly colored and larger than females. In species where males and females have the same plumage to the human eye, they can be quite different to birds that can see in the ultraviolet spectrum.

In some species of raptors like eagles, hawks, owls, falcons, and vultures, females are larger than males. With some like the Cooper's hawk, the size is noticeable as the female is a third of a size larger than the male. With others, it is not noticeable unless they are side by side or on a scale. This is known as reverse sexual dimorphism.

In the raptor world, females are larger than males. These are two first-year sharp-shinned hawks that were captured at a bird-banding research station. Note how much larger the female on the left is compared to the male.

Some birds like the common loon or the great northern diver, as it's known in some countries, have a challenging time with copulation. Their legs are so far back on their bodies that they're perfect for swimming underwater, but useless for walking on land. The birds squirm their way to shore, and the male tries to heave his body onto the female. After wiggling his tail around her tail for copulation, he slides off over her shoulder and tries to quickly return to the water.

When gathering mud for nests during the breeding season, cliff swallows will flutter their wings above their heads to prevent unwanted copulation. Both males and females need to do this because the initiator of the copulation sometimes doesn't care if he mounts a male or a female.

Bird Flirting, What the Ladies Are Looking For!

What do we want when it comes to finding a mate? It's not an easy answer because we all desire different qualities in the person we share our lives with on a day-to-day basis. I may find the quiet, nerdy type who works on the home with me attractive, but someone else may prefer to find an older male with a large cache of food and a beautiful home more desirable. Others may want to raise some offspring but do not want to deal with the hassle of finding a partner to live with long-term. Like us, different birds have different qualities that they look for in a partner.

SOME WANT A GOOD PROVIDER

When a male great horned owl tries to attract a mate, he will cache dead prey in hidden areas in his territory. Once he has attracted a female with his territorial hooting, he will immediately present prey presumably to show what a good provider he will be as a mate.

Northern cardinals appear to kiss during their mating display. The pair will call softly to each other back and forth, but the female is soliciting a male as if she were a young bird. That kiss may actually be a test to see how responsive he will be to their offspring.

Males who increase their presentations of caterpillars at mealtime turn on female blue tits. When extra food is presented, it stimulates the female to lay eggs.

A male emperor penguin probably gets the award for the most devoted dad. After the female lays the egg, she leaves it to the male while she returns to the ocean to swim and gorge on food for the chick. The male must incubate the egg, balancing it on top of his toes and never letting it touch the ice. If the chick hatches before the female returns, he can produce a milk-like substance on his limited fat reserves. When the female returns, he will finally leave to feed himself. She may have been gone up to four months, and he may have lost up to 50 percent of his body weight.

Many species of terns like the common tern and the Caspian tern incorporate food into their courtship rituals. A male does not get access to the female until he presents her with a fish.

SOME WANT A GUY WHO CAN SING

American bittern males inhale air in deep gulps and then gradually release the air in an undulating "song." Some may find his music akin to a pump churning water, and female bitterns find it irresistible.

Some species of thrush like the wood thrushes and hermit thrushes have the ability to sing two notes at the same time because of the way their syrinx is shaped.

Don't let the simple brown plumage fool you. What the hermit thrush male lacks in color, he makes up for in song and he has the ability to sing more than one note at a time.

The American Bittern's water pump call makes them the Tom Waits of singers and proof that there is someone for everyone.

Male kakapos walk to the higher elevations in their breeding territories in New Zealand. He will scrape a depression into the ground and sit there while giving his deep booming call to attract a female. The sound can travel as far as three miles.

The superb lyrebird is an Internet celebrity for his vocal abilities thanks to David Attenborough. Female lyrebirds are suckers for a good impressionist. The male creates a stage by clearing an area and learning the sounds around him, from kookaburras to cameras and even chainsaws. Some lyrebirds sing birdcalls that cannot be identified. Since they learn their songs, it is possible that older generations learned the songs and sounds of extinct generations, and we are hearing ghosts from the past in their courtship displays.

There will always be girls, like female woodpeckers, who go for the drummers. Their type of territorial drumming, for example, can even identify some species. The yellow-bellied sapsucker male starts fast and slows toward the end. Sometimes drumming causes males to become a nuisance, as the males like to find a dead hollow tree to carry the sounds for miles. Alas, some woodpecker species find aluminum siding or metal pipes on houses the perfect resonator, much to the chagrin of the homeowner.

It could be said that Adélie penguin females are chubby chasers. Research found that females listened to the calls of males and the choice males were the fatter ones. There was so much fat around the male's voice box that it created a more sustained pitch. A nice fat male would be less likely to abandon a chick to feed himself while the female was out gathering food.

SOME FEMALES ARE LOOKING FOR A GUY
WHO CAN DANCE

The red-capped manakin
is one of the most famous birds
on the Internet and well-known
for his ability to "moonwalk"
to attract females.

The red-capped manakin has earned the nickname "the moonwalking bird" for his ability to shift backward on a branch like the late King of Pop.

One of the rarest birds on the planet is the marvelous spatuletail, a hummingbird with a tail longer than the actual bird. Two incredibly long feathers lead from the body and end in fat tufts. When a female is present, the male will flit back and forth in front of her using his wing beats to float the ends of the tail above his head. This is an exhausting endeavor that is often lost on the female audience but never ceases to wow humans.

Cranes are a bit like a Hollywood musical during courtship by singing and dancing. Pairs leap up off the ground and bellow out their strange trumpet-like call.

Male ruddy ducks do a water dance to get the female's attention. They start by rakishly lifting feathers on either side of their head erect. Then he inflates his neck and beats his bill against his chest, intensifying in a bubbly crescendo and belching sounds. Nine out of ten female ruddy ducks find this incredibly hot.

Flamingos dance in large groups. The male and female appear to have the same moves but will dance in synchronicity with as many as fifteen to fifty flamingos. Some studies suggest that the groups of dancing influence groups of birds to lay eggs at the same time, which could be a way to maintain a larger flock and safety from predators.

Long-tailed manakins engage in a leapfrog-type dance, trying to outjump the other in order to impress a female. It's not the length of the tail that matters to her, but how well he jumps.

They may not be the prettiest birds out there but even turkey vultures try to work a little dance in when tempting a female.

Even vultures are not afraid to get their groove on when it comes to attracting a mate. Turkey vulture males will begin by holding their wings out and then rocking back and forth. During the dance, the male inflates red air sacs around his chest while giving a low grunting sound. It may not be pretty to us, but the lady vultures dig it.

Albatrosses perform some of the most elaborate mating dances of birds on the planet. Laysan albatrosses have a complicated ritual that involves head shaking, bill tapping, sky pointing, singing, and bill clapping. Sometimes a third bird will join in, but the dance is so elaborate that the monogamous pair only has eyes for each other.

The jury is still out on whether blue-footed booby females like a dancing male or if they just have a foot fetish. The male's dance consists of exaggerated steps, showing off his sky-blue webbed toes. Even after copulating, the male will flaunt his toes at her for the chance for another go.

Males can get overzealous when confronted with a hot female.

BIRD BUSTING!

Bald eagles mate in midair.
People often remark about the majesty of bald eagle mating and how the birds mate in midair by grasping talons and swirling downward in the heat of passion. That's not copulation; that's actually just foreplay. Bald eagles may not actually copulate in midair, but there's evidence that some swift species are able to mate in midair. Generally, birds do it while perched.

LET'S FACE IT, SOME LADIES WANT ACROBATICS

Female woodcocks watch the males do a wild and spinning flight display just after sunset to choose who they will mate with. No one know exactly what criteria the females are searching for in a male, but the display is a popular springtime activity for many bird-watchers.

Male woodcocks begin their display fifteen minutes after sunset, tumbling and spinning in the air, culminating in a spiraling flight, and landing on the ground. No one knows for certain what qualities the females are searching for during his flight. Woodcocks do not need this flight for foraging; the males only do it during the breeding season.

Bald eagles will grab their mate's talons in midair and spiral down toward the ground. Most of the time, both birds let go and fly away to continue the foreplay on a branch. On a few occasions, some birds get lost in the moment and fall to the ground.

White-throated swifts also engage in a courtship fall similar to bald eagles and have been documented plummeting five hundred feet. The birds rarely hit the ground. It is unknown if actual copulation takes place, but copulation has been witnessed at the nest site, so it is unlikely.

Prairie chickens will display to the point of exhaustion. Males will dance by pounding their feet to the ground and charging one another. The dancing frequently leads to fights and this will go on for hours into the morning. Some standoffs between males will even end with the males facing each other aggressively and then dozing off until a female arrives to select a breeding partner.

What horned larks lack in color, they make up for by hovering in the air for long periods of time.

Many birds that are brown or gray will sing beautiful songs and then add a little flair by flying high and hanging in the air while they sing like the Eurasian skylark, brown-backed solitaire, and horned lark. The Sprague's pipit does this as well, but when he is finished, he drops like a stone from the sky in a dramatic stoop.

Rollers like the European roller or lilac-breasted roller get their names from their courtship display. Males perform spectacular dives during the breeding season, including rolling as they descend.

Blue bird of paradise males take their display to another level by hanging upside down and fanning their feathers. As if the blue alone of his plumage weren't enough, he's not truly appreciated until a female has seen all sides of him.

SOME GUYS MAKE THEIR BODIES SING

The tiny club-winged manakin snaps his club-shaped feathers on his wings together, producing a high-pitched song as his wings point up. It's loud and the ladies love it.

Ruffed grouse males seek out a large log for their courtship display. They stand atop the log and beat their wings against their body, producing a low drumming sound. Humans almost feel it more than hear it. Female grouse can rarely resist a drummer.

Both common snipe and Wilson's snipe fly high into the air and vibrate the feathers on their tail because some ladies just can't resist a guy who can really shake his tail feathers. The sound is more of a winnowing and to some, sounds monkey-like.

Some nightjars like whip-poor-wills perch and whistle their song all night long. Others like the common nighthawk perform a deep dive while angling their wings to make a booming sound with their feathers.

SOME WANT A FANCY DANCER AND A SNAPPY DECORATOR

Male satin bowerbirds use a combination of decorative hoarding and dance to woo females. His strategy will incorporate more dance or decoration depending on his age and the female's response. Younger females can be deterred by his exuberant dance and so over time, he incorporates more color into his nest display.

Frigatebird females like a big pouch and they cannot lie. Male magnificent frigatebirds inflate a large, bright red throat pouch like a balloon, then proceed to make grunt-like belching sounds to attract a mate, proving that there truly is someone for everyone on this planet.

American white pelicans literally get horny during mating season. A small horn grows on the top of the beak of both the male and female. The horn falls off about the time the birds begin incubating eggs.

Both sexes of American white pelican grow a horn on the top of their beaks at the start of the breeding season. Made of similar material as fingernails, the horn falls off not long after the birds mate, and no one is certain of its function.

The Temminck's tragopan is not afraid to let it all hang out to get a female's attention. He starts by standing next to the female and shifts his weight to one side, and then the magic begins in what scientists call the "full frontal display." He puffs up his feathers, whips his head back and forth, and then a blue lappet on his face grows and grows and grows until it's almost the full length of his front.

Fidelity in Birds

The big question everyone wants to know is, do birds mate for life? Some do and others do not. It depends on the species, how long it takes to raise young, and if it's worth it staying together for the long haul. If it takes several weeks or months to rear a chick or if you only have one egg at a time, pairing for life or at least several years makes sense. But if a bird lays as many eggs as possible in a season, spreading the genetics around with multiple mates may be a better solution to producing the strongest offspring.

An estimated 90 percent of all bird species are monogamous if you define monogamy as one male mating with one female and it lasts for at least one breeding season. Some birds may only keep the bond together for one season, a few for several seasons, and a handful of species for as long as they or their mate lives.

Pigeons are one of the few species who do pair up for life.

Black vultures are surprisingly monogamous. Perhaps that compensates for their appearance.

Bald eagles are one of the few birds to pair up for life, although some studies would indicate that they are more attached to the territory rather than the other bird. For example, a female eagle in Ohio lost her mate and found a new male a mere four days later.

Some people may refer to them as "rats with wings," but pigeons actually mate for life. What's the secret to a long-lasting relationship? For the male pigeon, it's regurgitating into his partner's begging beak.

Researchers studying dark-eyed juncos (see photo) found that females who had affairs outside of their mate had more grandchildren than loyal females. Sons hatched of the outside mate were likely to become philanderers themselves.

Male dunnocks incorporate pecking a female's cloaca as part of the courtship display. The pecking is to stimulate her cloaca to spew any sperm from a male that may have just mated with her. He waits to get the "all clear" signal and then mates with her.

Black Vultures are very monogamous. DNA finger-printing of thirty-two adult breeding birds and their thirty-six young found no evidence of any hanky panky. All the chicks in the nest belonged to the parents tending them.

Though clay-colored sparrows have been documented as monogamous on their breeding territory for a nesting season, females rarely return to the same breeding territory in subsequent years. Males are very loyal to the territory and will happily pair up for a season with whatever female shows up to breed.

One in ten mute swan pairings will end in "divorce."

🪶 Australasian gannets are probably the closest to humans when it comes to pairing up for life. The divorce rate of paired birds between mating seasons is 40 percent.

🪶 Because of their beauty and grace, swans have long been considered as a symbol of long-term relationships. However, studies have revealed that 5 percent of whooping swan pairs and one in ten mute swan pairs end in divorce. Don't worry, Bewick's swans still seem to take till death do us part seriously by rarely separating.

🪶 Bird divorce can happen for a variety of reasons much like human divorce. Female black-capped chickadees may trade up for a male with higher social standing.

🪶 Divorce doesn't always lead to a better life. Research has shown that 32 percent of female red-billed gulls in an area with few males may never breed again.

🪶 On the southeast Farallon Islands, if a female western gull lost her mate, she was not able to replace him, but a male can replace the female fairly quickly.

Same-Sex Pairings

Like humans, bird relationships can be complicated and not always black and white. Scientists have learned some interesting things about birds in zoos and in the wild and who they partner up with to raise chicks.

Over 130 species of birds have been documented engaging in some sort of same-sex activity and it often depends on which sex takes care of the chicks. Female birds that do a majority of the chick rearing rarely engage in homosexual behavior. Females that have less parenting duties have higher rates of homosexual activity; the same goes for males too. Biologists at the University of Newcastle in Australia found that male homosexual activity was more common in polygynous species of birds and lesbian pairings were more prevalent in monogamous species of birds.

There was a famous pair of gay chinstrap penguins at the Central Park Zoo named Roy and Silo who paired up in 2004. The two males were so intent on raising a chick, one was observed rolling a rock to their nest and both spent time incubating it. Keepers eventually gave the pair a fertilized egg and they successfully raised her to adulthood. Silo eventually left Roy for a female in the tank named Scrappy.

The percentage of birds of a particular species suggests that for some, this is their strategy for survival and raising young.

Researchers studying laysan albatrosses on Oahu discovered that almost a third of the birds nesting on Kaena Point were involved in lesbian pairings. In 2004, 39 of the 125 nests were genetically tested and found to belong to female-female pairs. Though albatrosses mate for life, lesbian pairs still found willing males to fertilize eggs for their nest.

Nearly a quarter of black swans are in same-sex parings. In some cases, males in homosexual pairings will mate with a female, chase her off after she lays eggs, and rear them on their own.

Some studies on white ibises suggest that mercury may be affecting mate selection.

Many know that chemicals had an affect on eggs of peregrine falcons, but some studies suggest the chemicals from pollution may affect mate selection in other species.

Twenty percent of graylag geese are in male homosexual pairings.

Another startling discovery was that in certain species, pollution affected the birds' sexual preferences and how they paired up. This is not true for all bird species but in a few water birds, mercury and DDT were a factor.

A study in Florida found white ibises that consumed methylmercury, the most toxic and easily absorbed form of mercury found in the environment, were more likely to engage in same-sex pairings. The main sources of mercury globally are coal-fired power plants and gold mining, though in Florida, mercury was likely to have been released by the burning of medical and municipal waste.

Studies of injecting gull embryos with DDT, similar to the levels in birds of the 1970s, caused the development of ovarian tissues and oviducts in male embryos. The feminization of male birds may explain why there was a higher prevalence of lesbian pairings among female western gulls on the Santa Barbara Islands in Southern California.

In the 1970s, male western gulls mated with and then abandoned females. The unpaired formed lesbian pairs. After DDT was banned and chemical companies stopped disposing their waste into California waters, the sex ratios started to balance out.

Polyamory

They say it takes a village to raise a child. With birds, it can take a flock. Certain species have developed strategies for chick survival that do not fit the traditional family roles that we have as humans.

The odds are good that the male bobolink you are watching sing in the spring is keeping more than one female in a nesting way.

Male bobolinks can be either monogamous or polygamous depending on the quality of their habitat. A male with a good habitat is strongly polygamous. In a Wisconsin study, 62 males were watched. Of those, 36 were polygamous (24 males pairing with 2 females, 11 males pairing with 3, and 1 particular stud with 4 females). Only 12 were in monogamous pairings and 14 failed to pair altogether.

Northern cardinals are considered socially monogamous but polygyny has been observed. Perhaps there's an unmated female hanging out or it could be that the male assumes the female in the neighboring territory is alone.

When they are singing their loud, "konk-lareeeee" call, male red-winged blackbirds are soliciting for a little something on the side.

🪶 Female spotted sandpipers compete for multiple males as their mates. The males do most of the incubation and brooding.

🪶 Male red-winged blackbirds are not monogamous. As many as fifteen females may breed and rear chicks in the territory of one male.

🪶 Emu males may be polygamous but they are the sole incubators and rear the chicks on their own.

🪶 Male ostriches perform a mating dance to attract several females to his harem. Though there will be one dominant female to the harem, he is free to mate with all the females in his territory.

🪶 Montezuma oropendolas have a type of harem system. Up to 130 females will build nests in a tree and like women, will get on the same cycle. Groups of females are ready to copulate at the same time and tend to build their nests on the same branch. One male needs to pick the branch with the fertile females to gain exclusive access to mating with them.

Feminist Birds

Not all females are looking for a male for the long term. Some just want to be fertilized and do the rest alone. A few just want to lay the eggs and move on.

In prairie chickens, males display by dancing on their booming grounds, also known as a lek. Groups of females arrive to choose the best male. The best male in the lek is referred to as a "master cock" by scientists; the lead female is known as the "alpha female" and chooses the master cock of the lek and all the lesser females follow her lead to mate with him.

Phalarope females take the mating game to a whole different level. Unlike other bird species, the female is more brightly colored than the male, displays to attract a male, and defends the territory. After she lays her eggs, she begins her migration south and the male stays behind to rear the young.

When a female northern jacana dies, females in surrounding territories will take over her area and her males. If the dead female had a mate who was taking care of her eggs, the neighboring females will destroy them and force the males to incubate a new set of eggs.

Female ruby-throated hummingbirds (see photo) are only interested in males for the copulation. After the act is complete, she drives the male out of her territory, builds the nest, and raises the chicks on her own.

This female Wilson's phalarope is more colorfully marked than the male. She's very independent; after laying her eggs, she will leave and the male will incubate and raise the young without her.

Artificial Insemination

Due to the popularity of ostrich and emu meat, humane artificial insemination techniques were developed at the University of Western Australia. Collection of ostrich semen involved creating a dummy ostrich for the male to balance on. Emus do not need this and will easily deposit their semen in a fake cloaca held by a human collector.

When the peregrine falcon was on the endangered species list, artificial insemination was key to the captive breeding program. Falconers trained male falcons to fly and deposit their semen onto a "semen collection hat," which was then deposited onto a female to lay eggs.

Some birds involved in captive breeding programs imprint on humans and attempt a mating. A famous example was a male kakapo which mated with Stephen Fry's cameraman for a BBC program.

BIRD BUSTING!

The barn swallow mourns its dead mate.
There's a very famous series of photos of a barn swallow mourning its injured mate that has been hit by a car and is dying in the middle of the road. The text with the photos reads that it is a male guarding its mate. But in reality, it's an adult mounting and mating with a dying young bird, even continuing sexual activity after the injured bird is obviously dead. Don't believe everything you see on the Internet.

A Tisket, a Tasket, Some Birds Would Do It in a Casket

wild turkey

In 1995, Kees Moeliker documented the first-ever case of necrophilia in mallards. A drake mallard hit the window of his office and another male proceeded to mount and mate with the corpse several times. The encounter lasted long enough for Moeliker to not only document the event but get photographs as well. Moeliker won a Nobel Prize for his documentation.

Experiments in the 1950s revealed that male wild turkeys would attempt to copulate with a female's head attached to a stick. An experiment was also attempted with a female body without the head and the males did not copulate with it. Nice to know that even a turkey is more interested in a female's head and not just her breast.

BIRD BUSTING!

Birds mate for life!

Most birds do not mate for life. Birds of prey are more attached to a territory, rather than the partner associated with it. If the same mate from last year shows up to the territory, that's great. If a new bird who would actually be considered a "grandchild" arrives for mating, that can work too.

Many birds species will pair up for a season, but even so, some birds will have affairs or what scientists call "extra-pair copulation."

What Can You Do to Set the Mood?

If you enjoy birds, naturally you want to be an excellent wingman and help them succeed in their breeding attempts. There are several things you can do to set up a hot meeting ground and encourage the males to succeed in their quest to carry on their gene pool.

The number one thing is to have a yard hospitable to nesting. Creating a nesting habitat is a big way to help your male feathered friends get a little loving from the females. A good habitat with lots of food and shelter makes a female feel safe and ready for mating.

TURN YOUR YARD INTO A HOT ALL-BIRD ACTION BAR SCENE

Providing nesting habitat is key. You can do that with plantings in your yard or you can create unique structures. This is a platform created at Bear River Migratory Bird Refuge. The refuge gets huge swarms of midges but doesn't have a lot places for swallows to nest, so an overhang was created for them to attach nests.

Avoid the use of pesticides and lawn care chemicals. These not only take away some of the insects many birds naturally eat, but can kill birds.

Build sturdy and predator-resistant birdhouses; hang gourds for martins or condos for colony nesting birds.

If birdhouses are not your style, plant trees and shrubs in your yard that birds like to nest in. These can be thick conifers or tangles of vines. Find out from your local nursery what native plants are the most suitable for your home.

Keep your cat indoors. Nothing kills the mood like a free-range cat that kills off your potential mate.

An important part of a female's diet during the breeding season is calcium for eggshell production. Birds are capable of finding sources naturally; for example, ducks will eat snails. But during the breeding season, offering oysters or eggshells can be a help. Since most people eat eggs on a regular basis, eggshells are handy. To prep them for bird feeding, either put them in the microwave for two minutes or boil them for ten minutes to minimize any risk of spreading salmonella. Crush them into a fine grit and either mix with birdseed or scatter on the ground. Don't worry; offering eggshells in winter will not cause female birds to lay eggs out of season.

Remember that the way to some female birds' hearts is through their bellies. Offering clean water and fresh bird food and can make most female birds ready for love.

This male pine warbler would welcome a nearby restaurant to help feed the family.

Consider offering "safe" nesting material for birds, usually natural fibers. This can be in the form of pet hair, yarn, or raw cotton. If you do offer yarn, cut it into strips that are no longer than six inches to prevent birds from becoming tangled during construction. In the summer of 2011, a woman found what she thought was a pair of conjoined American robin chicks. The vet who treated them discovered the young birds got tangled in plastic thread used as nesting material and the birds' wings became fused together as their skin grew around it.

Water, whether in the form of a decorative birdbath or in a small pond, is an excellent addition for birds like this linnet. It is essential to their survival and is handy in the construction of nests. This linnet takes advantage of a puddle.

Set the mood with a romantic bath! Birdbaths, fountains, and ponds are a great place for several bird species to meet. Some species of insect-devouring swallows build their nests of mud and saliva, and many males meet females that way. A clean water source is also part of good nesting habitat and certain to put a female at ease and ready for love.

HELP BIRDS FLIRT OUTSIDE OF YOUR YARD

Of course you want birds to get it on in your yard, but what about helping birds around your city or around the world? You can do a little or a lot, but it can all help birds.

🪶 A big mood killer is fishing line. This hard-to-see material is often lost in tangles by even the best-intentioned fishing enthusiast. Even if you don't go fishing yourself, always pick up discarded fishing line and throw it away if you can. Birds can die a slow and agonizing death if it gets caught on their feet or their beaks. Some birds even die by getting tangled to a branch while using it as nesting material.

🪶 Volunteer with your local nature and conservation society when they have days of cleaning trash and invasive weeds out of parks. These all help create a great habitat and is sure to encourage more mating in your community. Something as simple as an afternoon of pulling buckthorn from an area it doesn't belong in can go a long way to allow native plants for birds to feed and build nests.

🪶 If you live near coastal areas or prairie areas, find out from places like BirdLife International or your local conservation group if they need help with nest monitoring. Some birds like plovers nest right on the ground in highly populated areas and need wardens to help keep the public from stepping on the nests. If you are part of the solution to successful breeding, you are helping birds in a big way.

Vacation Ideas

Bird flirting can be witnessed in the backyard in the spring or on a pond in a local park, but for fun, consider a trip to watch lekking birds like prairie chickens, grouse, and snowcock. Several areas offer tours and opportunities around the world just to watch some of these spectacular displays.

United States
In the United States, Colorado and Oklahoma are home to the rare lesser prairie chicken. Woodward, Oklahoma, hosts the Leks, Treks, and More Festival featuring morning viewing blind trips for anyone to watch these birds dance and fight.

Other US states including Minnesota, Wisconsin, and Nebraska are just a few who offer blinds for viewing the great prairie chicken and its morning dance.

Guatemala
Book a trip to Los Tarrales in Guatemala to watch the jumping of the long-tailed manakin during their mating display.

North Wales
If you find yourself in North Wales during the black grouse breeding season, look into reserving a space on a game reserve or a taking a guided walk.

Papua New Guinea
If you want to watch the weird and spectacular displays of the birds of paradise, plan a trip to Papua New Guinea.

CHAPTER 7

Baby Birds

When you consider that birds are raising their family outdoors, it's incredible that anything survives. In watching birds through the nesting season, it's easy to marvel at the lengths some birds will go to in defending a nest, like watching a mockingbird dive repeatedly at a cat that is too close to a nest, but there is also heartbreaking brutality. You will frequently hear scientists caution that you shouldn't attribute human emotion to birds because they are completely different creatures who have brains that operate in a different manner than our brains. That is never more evident than when you witness some of the lethal parenting methods that birds use.

If you find a baby bird covered with feathers, it most likely does not need your help. It may be a ground nesting bird like a black lark or just learning to fly.

BIRD BUSTING!

That baby bird fluttering on the ground is orphaned and needs my help.
No! When baby birds flutter out of the nest, they need twenty-four to forty-eight hours to figure out how to use their wings and more importantly, how to land after flying. Many people see these smaller birds struggling to fly and incorrectly assume the parents have left, when 99.9 percent of the time, the parents are in a nearby tree scolding you, or simply laying low, trying to teach their chicks how to hide from humans.

Parental Learning Curve

For most birds, offspring are a kind of gamble. A common statistic is that 75 percent of the birds hatched in spring do not live to see the following spring. Baby birds have it tough. As soon as the chick is out of the shell, it is at risk from predators like snakes, foxes, and raccoons. But learning to fly is a tricky and dangerous business, learning to avoid cats and windows. For birds that migrate, there's the danger of flying into buildings, a lack of food, or illness. So, when birds lay eggs, many are trying to create as many offspring as possible at one time to guarantee that at least one will survive to adulthood.

Birds have to learn how to care for themselves before they can take care of young. That's why many birds of prey don't breed until they are in their third year or older, like in the case of eagles and albatrosses. The first batch of kids for many birds is kind of a practice round and if any chick survives, it's a miracle.

The first step is learning where to put the nest, and there is a bit of trial and error. Birds need to figure out a safe spot for a cup nest so a storm will not knock the nest down. It also needs to be a discreet location as to not attract the attention of crows and ravens who would be more than happy to rid the nest of its tasty contents. Inexperienced mallards will sometimes put a nest right next to a road or on the roof of a building, not realizing that she has to find a way to get her young to water after they hatch . . . and they won't be able to fly.

Birds also need to learn how to care for chicks and protect them from predators. If you watch a family of geese and see the adults far apart and the young all over the place, they will most likely lose their chicks to all sorts of dangers like predator fish, snapping turtles, foxes, and hawks. Experienced parents keep their gaggle of goslings in a tight group.

You can tell that this gray catbird has just left the nest recently. You can see traces of its yellow gape visible along the comb of its bill.

Incubation

Mammals carry their young inside as it develops. This is not practical for birds since many need to fly. The egg allows the chick to develop a little bit longer but not tax the female's resources. There is danger in that the egg must stay in one spot, but a well-constructed nest and attentive parents can make it work.

Some birds nest quickly. This European robin can get through the whole nesting process in about a month from the start of incubation to the day the kids leave the nest.

Incubation varies among species. In some, it is shared by both parents; in others, only one parent does it. This task is not only assigned to one sex. In a few cases, like Wilson's phalarope and ostriches, the incubation is done entirely by the male.

The shortest incubation period appears to be the house sparrow at ten to twelve days. The house wren comes in close at thirteen days. Even the smallest hummingbird, the bee hummingbird, takes fourteen to twenty-three days to incubate eggs. Most small garden birds fall in to this egg-warming time frame including chickadees, tits, cardinals, robins, and hummingbirds.

🪶 Great spotted woodpeckers incubate their eggs for ten to sixteen days, and rock pigeons incubate their eggs for about eighteen days.

🪶 Great blue herons incubate for twenty-seven to twenty-nine days. A hen mallard and Canada geese will incubate her eggs for roughly twenty-six to thirty days, almost a month of sitting still and keeping eggs warm. Since female ducks have no help from the male, they will cover the eggs before leaving to feed.

Osprey incubate their eggs for 34 to 40 days.

🪶 Raptors need a little more time to incubate their eggs. Barn owls sit on their eggs for twenty-nine to thirty-four days. Red-tailed hawks incubate for twenty-eight to thirty-five days. Bald eagles incubate for about thirty-five days. Osprey go a little bit longer and sit on their eggs for thirty-four to forty days.

🪶 A type of eagle called the bateleur incubates its single egg for fifty-five days.

🪶 The male emperor penguin incubates for the longest period nonstop, by warming the egg for sixty-four to sixty-seven days alone. Male kiwis will incubate for seventy-two to eighty days, but unlike the emperor penguin, the males will cover the eggs at night with leaves and sticks and forage for food.

What's Coming Out of That Egg?

This baby willet can run around within an hour of hatching; it is a precocial chick.

Some chicks hatch into this world naked, shaking, blind, and capable of doing nothing more than barely lifting their head and opening their beak as wide as possible. This type of chick is altricial.

Other chicks hatch into this world raring to go. Young wood ducks and hooded mergansers are able to leap from their nests and hit the ground running, following their mother to open water and swimming right away within twenty-four hours of hatching. Many shorebird species are like this too, and the young can even feed themselves, relying on their parents to guide them to food and shelter them from danger. This type of chick is called precocial.

When baby birds hatch, they have a tiny white notch at the tip of their beaks called an egg tooth that helps them crack open the shell. It disappears a few days after hatching.

This young pied-billed grebe is not quite ready to get his own food and insistently pecks his mother's head to get her to feed him small fish. Soon, he will be diving for food on his own.

Adults make sounds as they incubate; the young imprint on that sound. In many species, especially waterfowl, the young birds can be heard making soft and muffled pips from inside the egg.

When baby birds beg for food, their mouth or gape can be very colorful. This is kind of like a landing strip to tell parents where to put the food. In some species, the color will change slightly after being fed, giving the adult an idea of who was fed last.

Young owls will leave the nest before they can fly. This is called the "brancher" phase. Their feet are very strong and though they cannot fly, they can climb some trees if they happen to fall and land on the ground. Young owls can also change their shape, and if they feel threatened, they will puff out their bodies and spread out their wings, almost tripling in size to scare away a predator. They are almost more vulnerable to human intervention than predators. Well-intentioned people happen upon them and incorrectly assume the baby owl is abandoned. And since owls are masters of camouflage, you rarely find their parents who are almost always hidden nearby. The best thing is to appreciate the baby owl and then leave it alone.

This young green heron is barely out of the nest with the little bits of down still visible around its head. The bird now has to watch its parents and learn all their fishing techniques.

When most birds hatch, they imprint on what they see caring for them and providing them with food. They learn that this is what they will grow up to be and the parent is an example of who will be a rival for territory and what an ideal mate will look like. This is one of the reasons it can be a problem when humans try to raise a wild baby bird. If that bird imprints on humans, they are going to have a very confusing time during their first mating season. In captive breeding situations like with falcons and condors, puppets are used to feed the young, or in the case of cranes, technicians must use a full-size crane suit so the young birds will associate with other cranes and not humans when they are adults.

From Hatching to Adulthood

Small birds common in our backyards can get the kids out of the nest quickly. The turn-around can be so fast that in one breeding season, they can get out three or four broods. Blue tits and black-capped chickadees incubate for about twelve to sixteen days and then young leave the nest within about fifteen days after hatching—about a month turnaround!

Larger birds needs more time to learn to fly and leave the nest. Buzzards leave the nest at around fifty to fifty-five days, barn owls at around sixty days, and bald eagles can take anywhere from fifty-six to ninety-eight days to leave the nest.

This young northern flicker is the same size as his father, but the male is trying to show the young bird how to search for food. He will ignore his son's begging and fly to food sources, revealing where food can be found. This can be a long and noisy process.

Once a bird leaves the nest, it is as large as it's going to get. Some people will see a hawk flying around and think it's a baby eagle. If a bird can attain flight, it has attained its full length and size. In some species, especially birds of prey, the young are actually a bit larger because they are fat and sassy from good parents fattening them up for survival and their feathers are a bit longer than adults. Some scientists think young bird feathers are longer because they will be crashing around a lot and the feathers will go through a lot of wear and tear in the first year.

Birds that take a few years to grow into adult plumage help communicate to others of their kind when they are old enough and experienced enough to mate. It can also communicate that they are young and inexperienced and an older bird could push them around and take their food.

Young sandhill cranes stay with their parents until they are about ten months old. The family bond holds until the parents are ready to start their next breeding season.

On average, bald eagles do not start breeding until they are five years old, although, in some cases, it can be as young as four years or as old as seven.

Wandering albatrosses do not start breeding until they are between eleven to fifteen years of age.

Scientists and field biologists age birds in a very specific way. Every one hatched this year will get a birthday on January 1; they will be two years old, or in scientific terms, a Second Year or an After-Hatch Year bird. There are a few birds that can be aged by detecting slight variations in plumage to determine if they are Second Year, After Second Year, or even Third Year.

For the first two years, sharp-shinned hawks are brown on back with yellow eyes. When they are old enough to breed, they will be blue on back with bright red eyes.

So How Long Will These Birds Live?

It's a grim statistic, but roughly 75 percent of the birds hatched this year will not survive to next year. Life outside is hard. There are predators to evade, health to maintain, food to find, and for some, migration to accomplish. There's little room for error, and most birds have a terrible health plan. But if they can survive the crucial first year, birds can live to some spectacular ages. And thanks to the efforts of researchers who band birds, we can get an idea of ages.

NORTHERN CARDINAL BANDED 3-18-1997 FOUND DEAD 11-14-2003, AT LEAST 7 YEARS OLD

This cardinal was found dead at Carver Park in Minnesota. The bird had been banded by one of their researchers and the bird was at least seven years old when it died.

It's interesting to look through bird banding records turned in by researchers and biologists. It's also interesting to note that the fish-eating birds tend to live the longest. Two excellent resources for looking up bird ages are Euring (www.euring.org/data_and_codes/longevity-voous.htm) and the Patuxent Wildlife Research Center (www.pwrc.usgs.gov/bbl/longevity/Longevity_main.cfm).

The oldest known bird so far is a laysan albatross who was found alive at age sixty raising a chick on Midway Atoll in 2011. Albatross species tend to be long-lived, there are quite a few banding records of these aged birds. There's one that's over fifty-one years old and another that was found at forty-two years of age. At least three banded black-footed albatrosses were found to be over thirty-seven years old, and three banded wandering albatrosses have lived to be at least thirty years of age.

In the 1970s, a banded Arctic tern was found that was over thirty-four years old. Considering that it migrates pole to pole, that has to be one of the most well-traveled birds on the planet. The oldest great frigatebird found was forty-three years old, but there are least three others that lived well into their thirties. The oldest Atlantic puffin was just over thirty when it was found. And shearwaters are another long-lived species; several have lived into their thirties and forties but one particular manx shearwater was found alive just shy of its fifty-first birthday.

Young peregrine falcons must build up their wing muscles before they attempt flight for the first time. Young birds will perch on the edge of nest boxes and flap their wings to build strength. Peregrines have been known to live for nineteen years in the wild.

Large raptors can live well into their twenties and thirties. Some record holders include a thirty-two-year-old bald eagle, twenty-nine-year-old white-tailed eagle, a thirty-year-old red-tailed hawk, a twenty-nine-year-old honey buzzard, a twenty-eight-year-old great horned owl, and a twenty-year-old marsh harrier.

What about the birds in your backyard? They can live between ten to twenty years if they are wiley enough to evade predators. The oldest dunnock was twenty years old. The oldest European robin lived to nineteen years. It's possible for a blue jay to live well into its teens if it can survive the astronomical odds of leaving the nest alive. The oldest blue jay was seventeen. The oldest reed warbler was fourteen years; oldest American robin thirteen years; and oldest American goldfinch was ten.

BIRD BUSTING!

Anyone can raise a baby bird and successfully release it into the wild. No. Many countries require federal permits to take care of young and injured birds because extensive training is involved. A professional wildlife rehabilitator needs to be able to correctly identify the type of chick to give them the appropriate diet. For example, some birds eat mostly seeds and others eat insects. Too many seeds could kill an insect-eating bird. Also, can you teach a hawk how to grab and kill a mouse with its toes? I doubt it. Leave raising wild birds to professionals, or better yet, wild birds.

Diaper Duty

Nest maintenance is key. And if you have ever had a day at the office lamenting that you are not a bird, free to fly around and raise your kids, simply consider this: many songbirds have to carry their young's fecal material out of the nest . . . by carrying it in their beaks.

Birds that build large nests like hawks or herons have the ability to shoot out their poop to avoid soiling the nest. Eagles can sometimes shoot their poop out over six feet.

Hoopoes make their poop work for them. If danger approaches the nest, the young will aim and fire fecal material at the intruder. As if that weren't enough of a deterrent, the preening gland of the female and the young secretes some extra stinky oils, not unlike the smell of rotten meat, to make the nest smell as unappetizing as possible.

Some young birds vomit as a defense mechanism. Vultures, pelicans, gulls, and cormorants all will blow chow when approached by a nest intruder. Northern fulmars take it to another level by regurgitating a sticky oil from their stomachs. The oil is so tacky, it sticks to feathers and cannot be easily removed. Several species of predatory birds including herons, hawks, crows, and owls have been found dead as a result of feathers covered in fulmar gut oil.

A male eastern bluebird dutifully carries away a fecal sac (aka poop sac) from the nest. Human diaper duty doesn't seem so bad now, does it?

Parents of the Year

Some birds go to great lengths to care for their young, from defense against predators, or incubating eggs.

Mockingbirds are so aggressive in defending their nests that if they decide to nest near a bird-feeding station, they will not allow any birds to come near.

The award for dedication and endurance must go to the emperor penguins who attempt to raise their kids in the Antarctic. There are no materials to build a nest so the egg and young chick is warmed by overlapping fat on the top of the bird's toes. After the female lays the egg, she must return to the ocean to eat. She transfers the egg to the male's toes and he incubates it for another sixty days until the female returns. He does not eat and he endures the dark Antarctic winter surrounded by other males, huddling against wind that is sometimes over one hundred miles an hour. The females return right after the chick hatches to feed it, and she will have to cross hundreds of miles of ice from the ocean to return. That's dedication.

Woodcocks will stay frozen with the chicks hidden beneath them, using their cryptic feathers as a cover. They are so dedicated to this task that researchers who band them will use pointing dogs to find the female and simply reach beneath her to grab the young and tag them.

Killdeer are well known for their ability to pretend to be injured to lure a predator away from a nest or young, but so will certain species of ducks and warblers.

Common yellowthroats will flutter down off of reeds as if injured if you get too close to their nest.

A killdeer pretends to be injured to get your attention off its ground nest.

Birdie Dearest

If one of these egret chicks falls from the nest, the parents will most likely not feed it.

Some birds appear to be devoted parents while others are clearly playing the odds. Some species will try to lay as many eggs as possible, get them out of the nest quickly, and repeat in an attempt to get through two to four broods in a breeding season. Others may lay two or three eggs and once the first egg hatches, completely ignore the second egg. The second is a backup in case the first doesn't hatch.

Some bird species like robins, blue jays, and owls will continue to feed young if they leave the nest a little early or fall out. In a heron or egret nesting colony, it's out of site, out of mind. If a chick falls from the nest, the adults will not feed it. If the chick is lucky, it will have a quick death and be eaten by a passing coyote or fox. Otherwise, it will slowly starve to death.

Great blue herons will leave the nest when danger approaches, even if it is a raccoon that they could conceivably attack with their sharp bill. They will not attack the predator in an attempt to drive it off but sometimes even watch the carnage happen. This may seem heartless, but as long as the adult herons survive, they can always rebuild a new nest and start over.

If there is plenty of food, all three of these osprey chicks will leave the nest fat and happy. If food is scarce, the older and larger birds will outcompete the smaller and younger birds.

Sibling Rivalry

Though some parents will lay several eggs and try to raise as many as possible, if food isn't enough, the siblings will fight among each other. Incubation plays a role. Some species will not start incubating eggs until the female has finished laying them. Other species will incubate as soon as the first egg is laid, leading to chicks hatching on different days and much older siblings. If the adults do not bring enough food, things get ugly fast. If you have a rough relationship with your brothers and sisters, at least your risk of siblicide is much lower than it is in birds.

Great egrets will lay anywhere from one to four eggs, and it's rare for all to survive. Because the birds incubate as soon as the first egg is laid, the older birds will have such a head start and be much larger by the time the last egg hatches. The older birds will peck at and jab the younger, weaker ones to the point that they either die or get evicted from the nest.

The black eagle found in the Middle East and Africa has one of the highest rates of siblicide. One study covered two hundred nests, and of all of them, only one fledged two young. The adults do not interfere with the attacks made by the more aggressive and usually older chick, and the weaker chick usually dies from starvation or injuries sustained by the other bird.

Blue-footed boobies are beloved for their sky blue feet and goofy mating dance. However, life in the nest is not so comical. The chick that hatches first will attack the younger chick. If the adults do not bring it enough food, the older one will continue to pick on it and the adults may even drive the weaker chick from the nest where it will be pecked at by neighboring parents until it starves or is eaten by a predator.

The Good Siblings

Not all bird species are so cutthroat in the nest, some birds actually raise their young in family groups, with the young of the previous year aiding the parents to care for the youngest.

baby crow

Acorn woodpeckers live in family groups. Two or three females will pair up with a group of four to seven males and raise their young in the same cavity. If all the females are not laying eggs at the same time, some eggs may be destroyed by the other females until all of them start at the same time.

American crows will stay in the family unit for two to four years after hatching and aid in the chick-rearing duties. The younger birds do not start breeding themselves until they leave the family group.

BIRD BUSTING!

Every bird is eligible for Parent of the Year.
No, though many species go to great lengths of endurance beyond our comprehension, quite a few parents do nothing as older siblings pick on and eventually kill their younger nest mates.

Foster Parenting

Birds are not known for their ability to count. Because of this, wildlife rehabilitation professionals will often foster young birds in other nests since it is very difficult for humans to raise a bird without imprinting on humans.

Certain birds bargain on this inability to count as they have more eggs than they know what to do with and find other nests to accommodate them. For some, it is a case of too many eggs and not enough nest. For others, it is a matter of letting someone else do the work to raise the offspring.

Many species of waterfowl engage in "egg dumping." It can be a case of a young and inexperienced female that has too many eggs or no nest. In the case of wood ducks, it's not out of the question to have one or two hooded merganser chicks mixed in with the young. The hen usually doesn't notice.

In cases of cavity nesting ducks, if there are too many females in an area and not enough nest cavities or nesting boxes, egg dumping can be a real problem. Some nest boxes can have twenty to thirty duck eggs. There's no possible way for a hen to incubate all of those eggs successfully and many end up not hatching.

For some, like coots, it can be a sneaky way of spreading your offspring around. However, coots have shown the ability to count and in some cases, recognize that a chick hatched is not their true offspring. They have been documented attacking chicks in their brood that are not genetically from them. If there is enough food, the chick might survive, although endure rough treatment. If food is sparse, the chick will die. Adults will attack the perceived intruder to the point that it will no longer beg for food and starve.

In the Americas, cowbirds lay their eggs in other bird nests. Many bird-watchers are surprised to find a tiny yellow warbler feeding a young brown-headed cowbird chick that is twice the size of the parent. But the instinct in some birds to feed a begging chick in the nest is so strong, they can't help themselves even if the "baby" is bigger than the nest itself.

Female cowbirds have a bit of mafia attitude in their tactics. They will stake out several bird nests to drop their eggs. A study conducted on nests where cowbird eggs were removed from the host nest revealed that the female cowbird would return and destroy all the eggs in the nest, forcing the birds to start over so she can lay another egg.

Since the cowbird grows faster than the chicks of the host family, they have an advantage. If food is plentiful, some of the siblings will survive, if food is scarce, only the cowbird chick will survive.

Unlike cuckoos in the Americas, cuckoos in Eurasia and Australia are nest parasites. When a female cuckoo quickly flies in to deposit her egg in another bird's nest, she will remove one to disguise what has happened.

Freshly hatched cuckoos, though blind and naked, have a reflex response preprogrammed into them. When they feel something touch their backs, they push their bodies backward until the item is gone. This usually results in the eggs of the host family being pushed outside of the nest and insuring the cuckoo will be an only child and very well fed.

Most birds that parasitize other birds specialize in dropping their eggs in a specific nest. However, the common cuckoo is a generalist and the species will dump their eggs in a variety of other nests. Over time, individual females will specialize in specific nests, most likely learning which birds are the most successful at raising her young.

In North America, ring-necked pheasants are an introduced species and a very popular bird with hunters. Native greater prairie chickens are at risk because pheasants will dump eggs into their nests. Because the pheasants hatch faster and the prairie chicken will leave the nest when the first birds hatch, many prairie chickens will leave behind their own eggs and go off and raise pheasants. In areas where greater prairie chickens are in decline, this is a problem.

Coots can grow up with some issues, as parents can be very hard on chicks they suspect were dumped in their nest.

How You Can Help Baby Birds

If you have a cat, keep it indoors. Baby birds have not evolved over the years with cats. In most areas, cats are a new species to the ecosystem. A cat outside sees a bird as a disposable toy, not a source of food. Even if you manage to get that baby bird out of a cat's mouth, it needs immediate medical attention. Cat saliva will cause an infection in any wounds on the bird, causing it to die within twenty-four to forty-eight hours of being bitten.

Hang out bird feeders but not near the nest. There's a rumor that says you should not have bird feeders out in the summertime because birds will not eat natural sources of food. For the most part, parents teach their young to eat all sorts of food and to not rely solely on the handouts of humans. It's also fun to watch adults teach their young how to use the feeders and to watch a baby bird clumsily cling to a suet feeder for the first time. Just make sure to keep them a good distance from the nest; you don't want to attract the whole neighborhood to a bird's quiet home.

If you find a nest in your yard, it's okay to visit it every few days, but not every day. Give the birds their space and if you are just too curious, get a spotting scope and watch from a safe distance.

One way to figure out a nest location is to watch bird behavior. Have you ever noticed a bird chipping at you with a mouth full of food but it won't move? Chances are good you are near the nest and the parent doesn't want to risk revealing the location by going to it. Give an adult space if you notice this behavior so the kids don't go without food for too long. Perhaps if you watch with a pair of binoculars at a distance, you might find the nest location!

A bird that stares at you with a mouthful of food without moving like this Brewer's blackbird most likely thinks you are too close to the nest.

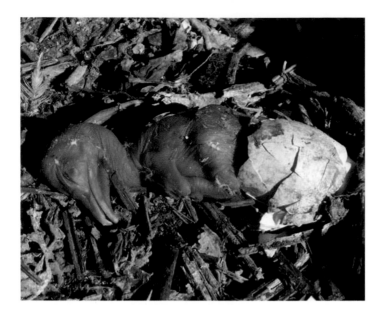

Many birds have specialized diets and should never be raised by anyone without the proper training and government permits. This baby pelican could not survive on bread and milk or even canned tuna. If you find a baby bird, it's best to leave it alone.

BIRD BUSTING!

Letting my kids raise baby ducks to release into the wild is a great science experiment for them.

It's certainly not good for the duck. Many places will sell baby ducks as a great temporary pet that can be released into the wild. Most ducks that are raised as pets and released into the wild are reduced to fox chow or coyote chow in less than a week. The challenge is that it's incredibly difficult to raise a bird around humans and not have that bird associate humans as a source of food. Also humans cannot teach a bird what a predator is and how to safely evade them. Another challenge is that some birds imprint on what they see feeding them when they are young. If a young bird sees a human feeding it, when it comes time for mating season, they will seek out other humans as a mate or defend their territory from other "rival" humans.

What to Do if You Find a Baby Bird

Unless it is in immediate danger of being hit by a car or killed by a cat, leave it alone. If the baby bird has no feathers, try to look around for the nest and put it back in. If the baby bird is covered in feathers, even if they are not fully grown out, do not put it back in the nest. Once a feathered baby bird has figured out how to leave the nest, they rarely stay there. The instinct to move and find cover will kick in.

If there is no immediate danger to the young bird, do nothing, let it learn how to fly and how to forage. Even if it can only flutter a few feet, let it be. It's hard work figuring out what those large appendages on the side with sudden feathers poking through your skin are for.

Unless you see blood or if you saw that baby bird in a cat's mouth, it does not need medical attention.

A baby bird's best chance at survival is to be raised by its parents rather than humans. This young osprey will still be tended by its family group.

Do not attempt to raise a bird on your own. In most cases, it is illegal, and if you do not have the specialized training, it can be very difficult. Different species have different diets. You don't want to feed an insect-eating bird a seed diet. Many think bread dipped in milk is good for all baby birds; it's one of the worst things to feed them, as they do not naturally digest milk, and bread has very little nutritional value. Only an experienced rehabilitator will be able to identify a young bird because many baby birds look very little like what they will grow up to be.

If you need to find help, it's easiest to look on the Internet for someone who specializes in rehabilitating wildlife. You can search for "find a wildlife rehabilitator near you" or type in "wildlife rehabilitator" with the name of your location. Be prepared to drive a couple of hours away and transport the bird yourself; most people who do this are volunteers and have little money and a large workload.

However, the best bet for the bird's survival is to leave it alone in the wild. The parents are going to hide from you to teach their young how to react around humans and also, they are trying to teach the young bird how to find food on its own. You may have to watch that baby bird for over an hour from inside your home before you see a glimpse of an adult. Even longer if it is a bird of prey like an owl or hawk.

I know these great horned owl chicks are adorable. However, raising a baby owl without the training and proper permits is in the Worst Ideas Ever Hall of Fame.

Venice Rookery, Florida

This is a great spot for the casual bird-watcher or nature photographer to get shots of young wading birds. Located in Venice, Florida on the west side of the state about an hour and a half drive south of Tampa, this spot will get you looks at nesting herons, egrets, ibises and wood storks. These birds are big, obvious and some are down right weird looking so it's a delight for both casual bird-watchers and the well seasoned hard-core birder.

Midway Atoll

You may have to sign up for a research project to get there, but if you have some time on your hands and can be flexible with your finances, Midway Atoll will give you crushing looks at 19 species of seabirds. It's an unorganized, unincorporated territory of the United States and maintained by the U.S. Fish and Wildlife Service. You have to apply for a permit to get there, but if you can you could find yourself among boobies, tropic birds, albatross and shearwaters. The oldest Laysan albatross on record breeds there and as of 2012 she was still raising chicks at 61 years of age!

Staycation Via The Internet

Not everyone can travel around to find baby birds, but the Internet can take you to them. Thanks to advances in outdoor cameras, you can get an intimate view of nesting birds from barn owls, to herons, to blue tits to bald eagles. Type in your favorite bird name along with the terms "nest cam" and chances are good that you will find a live video feed you can follow any time of day. Some of the most popular ones include the Decorah Eagle Cam on a family of bald eagles or the Cornell Lab of Ornithology's heron cam on a great blue heron rookery. Keep in mind that conditions are harsh and you may find yourself watching tragedy as chicks do not always survive.

CHAPTER 8

Cliff's Notes of Birding

Some people feed birds and are content to leave it at that. Others may want to actually go to parks or connect with birding clubs to meet other birders. Some may even go as far as to plan a vacation around a bird-watching festival. So long as you are not wiping out an entire species, your enjoyment of birds is your own. If you only want to count red birds, that's great. If you want to keep a list of how many birds you see in your state in one calendar year, that's awesome. If you want to track every single bird you see in every county and have the largest backyard list and even keep a list for your dog, that's your choice. It's all good, so long as you are not harming the birds.

Bird-watching is a relatively new pastime. If you think of life in the previous centuries, people had a lot more to do to maintain a home and raise a family so taking a moment (and extra money) to notice what was flying around outside for enjoyment wasn't possible. If they did notice birds, it would be large ones with an eye toward eating it or scaring it away to keep it from damaging crops.

For naturalists and artists who did study and document the birds around them, they were hampered by a lack of optics like spotting scopes or binoculars. In order to see a new or unusual bird up close, it had to be shot and killed. Then the feathers could be preserved or the bird could be sketched. If you have ever wondered how certain birds got their names like the red-bellied woodpecker because you can hardly see any red on the belly when it's alive and moving around in the wild, it's because the people who gave it the name shot a few. When the dead bird is only a few inches from your face you can see a hint of red on the belly.

Birds became a fashionable passion in the 1800s, but it was more for collections of the birds and their eggs. Because so much was learned from pursuit of these species and having them dead in hand, it was also considered a scientific study, though not everyone was interested in the collections process. Some just enjoyed shooting.

A huge and sometimes devastating hobby to birds was oology, the collections of wild bird eggs—these were the trading cards of their day. Men who would travel to remote islands to collect eggs were seen as adventurous scientists and rare species could garner a hefty price. We may look back and see it as barbaric now, but what do we do now that will be considered barbaric in a hundred years? Perhaps the practice of catching birds in nets only to place leg bands or satellite transmitters on them will seem cruel in the distant future.

Several factors came together for the creation of the Audubon Society. Founded in 1905, it was fueled by a grassroots movement of society ladies horrified to learn that the gorgeous hats they wore with lovely birds were the results of mass slaughters of large nesting colonies of birds and the voracious appetite for fashion was causing a serious decline in bird populations. The movement had started ten years earlier by sportsman George Grinnell who also wanted to stop the mass slaughter of birds. Though his early version of the Audubon Society didn't take, he was invited as an honorary vice president when Audubon incorporated in 1905.

One of the first books to encourage watching birds without a gun was *Birds Through An Opera Glass* by Florence A. Merriam. The book from 1889 encouraged readers to get the opera glasses out and, instead of using them to watch theater or their neighbors, to take note of the birds outside. The guide includes written descriptions of common birds, musical notes describing bird songs, and even a few black-and-white illustrations.

Many books in the early 1900s classified birds as either being good or evil, often based on whether or not you could eat them. The colorful language and descriptions makes them a fun read, especially in comparison to the drier language used in modern field guides. For example, Neltje Blanchan described the great horned owl as "the lord high executioner of the owl tribe" in her life histories book, *Birds That Hunt And Are Hunted*.

Roger Tory Peterson revolutionized identification guides and made them easy to understand, noting key features for identifying birds. Add to that the ability to use binoculars for observation instead of a gun, and bird-watching gained in popularity as a hobby.

Some oldies but goodies can be found when it comes to searching used book stores for older birding books.

Bird-Watching Terms

Once you start hanging out with other birders, they will use terms that will not only be confusing, but can sound down right dirty. Don't worry. They are actual terms, perhaps with unfortunate alternate definitions among teenagers.

Anthropomorphism: This can be a four-letter word to many hard-core birders. It means to attribute human emotions to animal behavior. Many scientists look down on the practice and since there is a blend between scientists and casual observers in the field, someone stating, "Look at those two eagles in love, playing together," might get a reprimand on the dangers of anthropomorphizing bird behavior.

Birding: Most bird-watchers prefer to be referred to as birders and their passion is birding, not simply watching birds. Their hobby includes studying behavior, volunteering for conservation, and engaging in citizen science projects like bird surveys. It's very similar to referring to a Star Trek fan as a Trekkie instead of a Trekker.

Digiscoping: This is a relatively new aspect to bird-watching and it's basically the technique of holding a digital camera up to binoculars or spotting scope to get photos. As cameras change, so has the practice. Some people attempt to get professional-grade photos holding a single lens reflex camera to a scope eyepiece, while others get great shots and video by simply holding up a smartphone to their binoculars.

Dipping: This is a British term that has worked its way over to the United States. It means missing the bird you set out to find. If someone asks if you saw the yellow rail and you didn't, you would answer, "Nah, I dipped."

Gripping: Another British term that means you saw the bird, but your friends did not. Showing off the awesome shots you got of a scarlet tanager to people who missed seeing it by ten minutes would be an example of gripping.

Jizz: This is a type of bird identification technique that should be spelled G.I.S.S. and stands for General Impression, Size, and Shape. So much of bird identification goes beyond the color of the feathers. Some species can be identified by wing shape, body movement like bobbing up and down, or its size in relation to other birds in the flock. G.I.S.S. is an air force term for spotting enemy aircraft but many birders prefer the alternate spelling of jizz birding, much to the delight of anyone who is familiar with the Urban Dictionary. I have seen teenagers spray soda through their noses when overhearing a seventy-three-year-old birdwatcher announce, "Well, the jizz of that bird reminds me of a young dickcissel."

Life List: This is the list you keep of all the birds you have seen in your entire life. There are many subcategories like a county list, a year list, a backyard list, and even a "this bird pooped on me" list. People who care more about getting a new bird on their list than a great view of a bird they have seen before are frequently referred to as Listers.

Lifer: A new bird that you just saw and can add to your life list.

Lister: Someone who is only concerned with getting as many birds as possible on their Life Lists. Typically, Listers are so focused on accumulating the ticks on their lists, that a simple glance at a bird for two seconds will suffice. You will sometimes hear variations like "Clister" or a County Lister.

Pishing: A sound a birder makes by whispering the word "pish." During certain times of year, birds will respond to this by getting closer. It's a way to get warblers to come out from a thick canopy. There's some debate as to why birds respond to it. One theory is that it sounds like a warning call and other species come in to join the mobbing of a potential predator. Another theory is that it sounds similar to a baby bird begging for food and since pishing is most effective during the breeding season, birds are so in tune to feeding young, they automatically follow the sound.

Ticking: This means to check birds off on your list.

Twitching: Is a European term that means to look for a reported rare bird. Some birders in North America use it interchangeably with birding or listing, but if you hear a British birder say, "I twitched the common yellowthroat in Gwent last year," that means they saw the report and made the trip to see it.

For more birding terms see page 273.

Even though this group had a long day of meetings ahead for the Changing the Face of North American Birding Conference, they made time to watch birds before it started. Birding in a group is a great way to make new friends and exchange tips for bird identification.

BIRD BUSTING!

All bird-watchers are ornithologists.
No. Many people can have an interest in ornithology or the study of birds, but it takes an actual degree, either a Masters or a PhD in zoology or biology with an emphasis in bird study, to call yourself an ornithologist.

Frustrating Bird Names

Bird names change a lot! As ornithologists learn more about bird origins through DNA studies, they are constantly changing bird names and taxonomy. Depending on the age of your field guide, some birds may be lumped together or split apart and put back together again. Some field guides may call them northern orioles and others will call them Baltimore orioles, it's confusing and will only get more so in the future.

When ornithologists decide a bird species needs to be split into several other species, this is called "arm-chair birding" and it means you got a new life bird without making a special birding trip. For example, the cackling goose, a very small version of a Canada goose is now a separate species where it used to be the same. Don't get too comfortable with arm-chair bird-watching; dark-eyed juncos used to be four species and now they are only one.

Bird names can also be confusing. Robins in Europe are not related to robins in North America. However, blackbirds in Europe are related to robins in North America but not to blackbirds in North America. Confused yet? When European settlers first encountered North American birds, they named the new birds they saw after what they resembled back in Europe. Though larger, American robins have an orange breast and brown back similar to the smaller European robins.

Buzzards are another confusing bird. In North America, it is a folk name for the turkey vulture, but in Europe, it's a type of hawk, very similar to the red-tailed hawk.

Sparrow hawk is a common name used for a small falcon in North America known as an American kestrel. In Europe, the sparrow hawk is actually a close relative of North America's sharp-shinned hawk. There are kestrels in Europe but they are much larger than the North American version and closer in size to the European sparrow hawk. When settlers first came to North America, the small kestrel was so close in size to the European sparrow hawk and so much smaller than the European kestrel, the name stuck.

It seems that by the time ornithologists made it to Central and South America, they did away with naming birds after the most obscure identification feature on their bodies and went the opposite direction and started naming them for behavior: black flowerpiercer, scaly-throated leaftosser, and lineated foliage-gleaner.

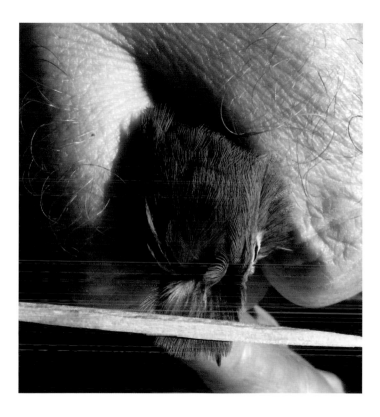

The orange-crowned warbler is an example of a bird that was identified and named by someone holding it in their hands. This drab bird appears to have no orange. However, if you hold one in your hand and use a toothpick to push forward the feathers on the top of its head, you can see a little bit of orange.

Who Are Those Guys a Lot of Birds Are Named After?

John James Audubon was an early bird artist who did one of the earliest comprehensive books illustrating the birds of North America. It could be argued that he was one of the first wildlife personalities as he also made quite a career out of presenting himself as a wilderness man as well as an illustrator. Audubon was frequently in debt and when he found a new species, he wasn't opposed to naming them after friends . . . or people he owed money to. His name is known for his early illustrations, the National Audubon Society and Audubon's warbler.

William Baird was a young protégé of Audubon's and become a great scientist in his own right. He was an associate fellow of the American Academy of Arts and Sciences and assistant secretary for the Smithsonian Institution. Several animals bear his name including Baird's sparrow and Baird's sandpiper.

Charles Bendire was a soldier, egg collector, and ornithologist. He discovered quite a few new species, noted habits of migrating birds, and discovered his namesake, the Bendire's thrasher.

Alexander Wilson was an ornithologist, poet, and illustrator who predated Audubon. There is some argument that Audubon blatantly copied some of Wilson's work. You will see Wilson's name all over the place in the birding world: Wilson's storm-petrel, Wilson's plover, Wilson's phalarope, and Wilson's warbler.

BIRD BUSTING!

John James Audubon killed a lot of birds.
Yes, he did! In his day, there were no binoculars and if you wanted to identify a bird species, and especially if you wanted to paint it, the bird had to be shot.

Types of Birding

Local birding is the most common type. Many birders get attached to their local patch, a park or private land that they visit whenever they can and keep track of what birds they see and when. If you have a good local patch that no one else uses very often, you do increase your chances of noting a rarity in your area.

Guided walks are generally offered by small nature centers and local bird clubs and can be used to better your bird knowledge and make new bird-watching friends. These walks also help give you an idea of what rules and protocols happen when out with a group.

Bird festivals are great for beginners and hard-core birders alike. They are especially handy when visiting an area that you are completely unfamiliar as the expert leaders will help you find the birds you seek. Always plan an extra day or two around a festival to give yourself a chance to revisit a favorite spot or seek out a bird you may have missed.

Birding tours are ideal for finding new species in a country where you do not speak the language or you have no idea how to find certain species. Some lodges that cater to birders even employ their own local guides. Definitely do some basic research on these companies online. It is rare but there have been a few smaller companies that have landed themselves in unsafe situations or landed the group in a town, but ran out of money to cover accommodations. Some of the larger guiding companies may even give you an opportunity to be in the field with some of your favorite bird-watching authors too, and who better to teach you about bird identification?

Competitive Birding

Many birders of all levels like to try a "Big Sit." Pick a spot and try to document every bird you see and hear in a twenty-four-hour period.

There are some events that turn bird-watching into a competition. Some nature centers or sanctuaries will host bird-a-thons where birders are given a set area and teams compete to see the most birds in a day. Teams gather sponsors who donate a set amount of money per bird found. The most famous competition is the World Series of Birding in Cape May, New Jersey, and teams from all the major optics companies, Cornell Lab of Ornithology, and bird-watchers of all kinds compete. Money raised from the event goes to a variety of conservation organizations.

Big years have been popularized, thanks to the movie *The Big Year,* based on the book of the same name. It's a personal competition to see as many birds in a year in a country as you can. There are several sorts of subcategories to this because some birders who cannot afford time off work or the airfare to fly all over the country limit their bird-watching to just their home state, town, or country. There's no big reward for this apart from self-satisfaction.

Big days are a smaller version of a big year, and it's similar to what happens in a bird-a-thon. Though depending on the size of the state, some birders will have to cover much more ground.

Big sits are relatively new and gaining in popularity. You sit in one spot for twenty-four hours and note every bird that passes by. You can also count birds heard and birds that fly away in the distance, but you can't move around. If you do it during migration, anything is possible.

Ten Rules Birders Wish You Knew Already

When you get into birding, you are excited to go out with others. But birders are a strange bunch and several unwritten rules have been established over the years. Not all birders have these rules, but these are common ones that pop up and surprise newbies in the field.

1. When birding in a group, do not use recorded calls or pishing without permission. Everyone has different guidelines for how they want to enjoy birds or get them on their "life list." Some want to do it without any use of a recorder; others don't care. If you want to attempt to get a bird to hop out of a bush and other birders are nearby, ask first.

2. Don't reveal owl nests. Seeing an owl in the wild is one of the things a birder lives for; they are one of the most coveted species to add to a list. However, some would argue that they should not be reported. And nothing starts an argument in the bird-watching community like asking whether or not an owl should be reported.

3. Do not wear white in the field. This is a newer rule based on a book of collected essays called *Good Birders Don't Wear White*. The thinking behind the book is that if you are birding in a wooded area, the bright white sticks out like sore thumb and makes the birds uncomfortable. This rule is debatable, but there are some field trip leaders who will insist that you wear subdued colors in the field.

4. You most likely did not see the rare bird. When new to bird-watching, it can be hard to find the bird you are looking for in the field guides. Perhaps in your limited abilities, the rarest bird possible is the one you think you have found. It's highly unlikely. It's true that birds do not always follow maps laid out in the book, but the chances that you had an ivory-billed woodpecker at your feeder are astronomical.

5. If someone offers you a chance to look through their scope, do it. Stand right behind them as they line it up. Generally, people with great optics like to share their view.

6. Don't be a scope hog. At the same time, if there is a line of people standing behind you to get a look at their first ever cream-colored courser, don't stand there for a whole minute, let others have the chance and then afterward you can try for another look.

7. Don't hold your camera up to someone's scope without permission. Digiscoping is all the rage right now for getting souvenir shots of birds in the field. However, without practice, it's a good way to scratch a $200 scope lens. Ask before you do this technique on someone else's scope.

8. Don't walk or stand in front of someone's view. This is a common faux pas in the excitement of seeing a life bird, especially in field-trip situations. Be conscious of your view—there could be shorter people behind you or a host of twenty scopes. Someone could also be taking photos or video, and it's not out of the question for someone to catch you blocking their view on video and post it on YouTube.

9. Obey "No Trespassing" signs. Even experienced birders ignore this sign, and it's bad news when it happens. It can cause normally tolerant security to ban all bird-watching access to a great spot. It is also inconsiderate to private property owners. No bird is worth violating a "No Trespassing" sign.

10. Give birds their space. Especially in the advent of digital photography, which grants anyone with the right amount of money the equipment to get shots of birds, sometimes we forget the bird's comfort and safety. Many digital photographers will work to see how close they can get to a bird in a full-frame shot, needlessly flushing the bird. Learn how to approach birds without flushing them.

Professional Birding

So let's say that you enjoy watching birds so much, you want to throw caution to the wind and give up that desk job and do it full time. Perhaps you are a young student and are considering birds as a career choice. Maybe nature photography is your passion and want to live the life. The jobs are few and far between and rarely pay well.

Ornithologist: This is a PhD in biology with an emphasis on bird studies. This can lead to a career in academia, as well as becoming a scientist and solving problems like wild bird management on properties, bird food development, species preservation, and wind farm placement. Some even specialize in fields such as forensics and can be experts in determining what sort of species got caught in aircraft and caused a crash.

Field Trip Leader: On the surface, this sounds like an exciting, travel-the-globe sort of job and it is. But keep in mind, you are on the road a lot and it is a competitive field. Also, there's a lot of pressure to find a variety of birds during each trip, and there will always be the disappointed person who missed the superrare bird that they paid all the money to see. Your trips can last weeks and you may not see friends and family for months at a time.

Nature Photographer: The quote I've heard is that the best way to make money with nature photography is to sell your equipment. As digital photography becomes more accessible and more people are able to capture great images, even with their smartphones, it's almost impossible to earn a full-time living with photography alone.

Bird Survey Technician: These are almost always temporary positions, usually from three to six months, and can take you anywhere from Alaska to South America or even to American Samoa. These jobs can involve tracking birds via telemetry, bird banding, nest monitoring, checking and identifying carcasses at wind turbines, and long lonely days in the field.

Bird study has a strong history in citizen science. Some of the most well-respected work done in the field has been by everyday people with a passion for birds. One of the first people to compile a complete life history record of every known bird species in North America was Arthur Cleveland Bent, a businessman who enjoyed birds as a hobby. He used his own notes and the notes of others to compile the first series of books to give us information on North American bird breeding, migration, and habitat requirements.

Bent's work is still referenced to this day and there are more than a few birders who raid used bookstores to look for bits and pieces of the series. Bent showed what someone with a passion and a head for research could accomplish. Even if you cannot afford to go into the less-than-lucrative career of birding, there are plenty of volunteer opportunities to do things like banding birds, document breeding records, or even sign up for volunteer vacations where you help lodges in other countries create wildlife friendly habitats.

Good birders should pay attention to how other people enjoy the outdoors and wear orange during deer season in the United States.

Birding Gear
Vacation Ideas

Bird festivals are a great way to learn about the hip bird watching life style. They are primarily held in North America and the idea is gaining momentum in other countries but for the moment, the United States holds some of the best events.

Space Coast Birding and Wildlife Festival

This January event is a welcome vacation idea for northerners. The festival brings top birding guides and authors to show you a fun an educational time identifying gulls at a landfill or tracking down endangered species like the Florida scrub jay and red-cockaded woodpecker. Because of the large crowds, there is a vibrant trade show and it's a great spot to look for new binoculars. Fantastic photographic opportunities abound as the birds are cooperative and the terrain is easy to navigate. This is near Orlando and Cape Canaveral so it can be tagged on to a visit to Disney World or Kennedy Space Center for the nonbirder in your life.

San Diego Bird Festival

This March festival gives you some great west coast birds, a chance to go on a pelagic trip to get some seabirds like fulmars, shearwaters, auklets, murrelets, and jaegers on your life list and even a few trips for desert species like verdin, phainopepla and roadrunners. This event also offers some unique trips to tempt a non birder with you like a birds and wine trip, birding by bike and even birding by photography. Because of it's location, it's a little more pricey than some festivals located in remote areas, but it is well worth it.

World Series of Birding

You can either gather a team or just kind of hang out around the town of Cape May, New Jersey, and enjoy the frenetic vibe of bird watchers scrambling to win such accomplishments as Most Birds Seen In 24 Hours, Most Birds Found While Riding A Bike In 24 Hours, Most Birds Photographed In 24 Hours, you get the idea. This event is used to raise money for conservation projects and is the oldest bird competition. Everyone should check out this birding craze at least once.

CHAPTER 9

The Hip, Birding Lifestyle

Compared to other hobbies, birding doesn't have quite the gear requirements as say fishing or hunting. As a matter of fact, it's possible to go "naked birding," going out with just your body—no notebook, no binoculars, no book. Back when I was a poor college student, I did a little bit of birding like this. However, birding is much more fun if you can see the birds well and have a means of documenting a bird you can't identify.

It always surprises me when people assume bird-watching is a nerdy pursuit. Watching birds is an adventure that takes you down the road less traveled and can be a total adventure.

Essentials that a Birder Needs in the Field

🌿 Binoculars

🌿 Spotting Scope

🌿 Notebook and Pencil

🌿 Water

You may wonder why a field guide isn't included on this list. Field guides are heavy and some of the best ones weigh over four pounds, though this can be solved by downloading an app or e-book version and storing it on a smartphone. However, the risk of having a guide with you is that you will spend more time looking at the book trying to identify a new bird, rather than actually watching it. A better way to learn identification is to take notes on what you see, maybe even try to do a rough sketch, and then consult your book in the car or at home.

BIRD BUSTING!

Bigger is better when it comes to binoculars!
You may think that getting binoculars that have twelve-power magnification or zoom up to twenty power will be better because it's going to make the birds appear closer. However, binoculars with high magnification are going to be sensitive pieces and will be hard to hold up. Often you will be shaking the image so much, it will make getting a clear view hard. As in many things in life, bigger is not necessarily better.

The numbers that you see on binoculars (8 x 42 or 10 x 50) have more to do with magnification and brightness. They do not define how wide your field of view will be.

A blank notebook is far more helpful in the field than a field guide. Sketching what you see gives you a permanent record of what you saw and helps insure you won't spend more time flipping through your field guide than watching the new bird that is right in front of you.

BINOCULARS

Choosing binoculars can be a daunting task. There are so many prices and size ranges and because no one binocular fits every single person's face, it is subjective.

What Exactly Do Those Numbers Mean?

All binoculars have an equation like 8 × 30 or 10 × 42. The first number gives you an idea of the magnification, or how close the bird will appear to you when you look through them. So an 8 × 42 binoculars will essentially appear to make the image eight times closer to you. A 10 × 42 will essentially bring the image ten times closer.

The equation on binoculars gives you an idea of the magnification and brightness the piece will give you.

The second number in the equation on binoculars is the diameter in millimeters of the objective lens, the large lens at the end of your binoculars. It does not mean how wide your field of view is, but it will give you an idea of how bright the image you see through your binoculars will be, which is essential on cloudy days or at dawn or dusk. A smaller objective lens will make your binoculars lighter but may not be as bright as a larger one.

Logic would suggest that you want the image to be as close as possible and you would want to get binoculars that are 12x or even a 20x. However, the more a pair of binoculars magnifies an image, the smaller the field of view will be, making it more difficult to figure out where to aim your binoculars. Also, when you are working with higher magnification, it will be more sensitive to any shaking or vibration you give off. If you have a couple of cups of coffee in the morning, chances are you will notice a slight shake when you hold up your binoculars to your eyes. If you shake too much, it will make viewing the bird hard.

You will find similarly sized binoculars with wildly different prices. You can find an 8 x 42 for as little as $20 or even higher than $2,000. Different companies use different glass, delicate techniques of cutting glass, and even coatings on the glass to achieve maximum brightness. Do you need a $1,500 pair of binoculars? It depends on how often you use them. If you are someone who is only interested in the birds in your backyard and only go to a park to watch birds once or twice a year and only on sunny days, inexpensive binoculars will serve you well. If you are someone who goes out to see as many birds as you can, as often as you can, and are not adverse to bird-watching in the rain or in the predawn hours, the high-end binoculars are worth every penny.

BIRD BUSTING!

Binoculars must be worn around your neck.
False! One thing that can ruin a day of bird-watching is discomfort. Shoulder harnesses are the best thing to happen to bird-watching since convertible pants. They take the weight off of your neck and distribute them to your shoulders. They also hold them securely in place and free up your hands so you don't have to deal with that uncomfortable feeling of them bouncing on your chest. Pro Tip: When purchasing a new pair of optics, ask the store if they will throw in a harness for free—they almost always do.

SPOTTING SCOPE

A spotting scope has far more magnification than binoculars. Because of the high magnification, it must be set on a tripod to keep it stable. When scopes first came out, they were intended for hardcore birders who wanted to study gulls, shorebirds, waterfowl, and distantly migrating raptors. They were ideal for being planted in one spot and searching for birds at a distance. As scopes have advanced and become much lighter in weight, more birders are using them all the time. They are now a staple in a birder's arsenal, especially for their photography potential.

In cheaper scopes, you can get an entire package of scope, eyepiece, and tripod for between $300 and $500. They do the trick, but if you even look through a high-end scope, you will weep at the quality you've been missing.

High-end scopes usually sell the pieces individually; the scope body is separate from the eye piece and the tripod. Eyepieces can come in different magnifications like a 30 power fixed (it brings the image 30 times closer to you) or 20 to 60 zoom (it can bring the image 20 to 60 times closer to you).

Like binoculars, high-end scopes will have better quality glass and coating, making the clarity unbelievable.

A lot of people balk at taking a heavy scope in the field; part of what makes them so heavy is the tripod. You can now purchase carbon fiber tripods that make the scopes incredibly light.

A high-end scope with a carbon fiber tripod can run between $2,000 and $5,000. They may not be for everyone, but for people who plan to go out at all hours of the day and want to see as many birds as possible; these scopes are worth every penny.

There are also adaptors that will allow you to attach your spotting scope or large binoculars to your car window. This is especially handy for auto tours. Birds typically are not afraid of a slow-moving car, just the people inside it. It can be a good way to get close to different species and a scope on your window can get you up-close views and allow you to get photos.

DIGISCOPING

Using a digital camera with your spotting scope or binoculars allows you to take home great souvenir photos of the new birds you see.

In the last decade, the combination of a digital camera used in conjunction with binoculars and spotting scopes has gained in popularity. The combination trend started with using point-and-shoot cameras with scopes and binoculars, but as digital photography gained in popularity, many scope manufacturers made adaptors to secure the cameras firmly in place.

Digiscoping started as a means of documenting rarities, but as digital single-lens reflex cameras have become more accessible, you can get some quality shots with this technique. Now many cameras also allow you to take high-definition video.

Even crazier is that most smartphones will take quality photos and HD video. It's possible now to hold a phone up to a spotting scope and take a photo of a rare bird.

What to Ask
When Purchasing Optics

Can I try these out? The first step is to try out several kinds. When out watching birds with friends, ask to hold their optics and look through them. Note which brand of binoculars feel good in your hands and are comfortable to your face. Ask what the binocular owner likes or dislikes about them and listen carefully. Often, bird-watching events will have optic reps on hand who will loan out binoculars for people to test drive on field trips. Once you have a great pair of binoculars in your hand, you won't want to let them go, and the reps know that.

Are these waterproof? Most binoculars are now waterproof, even the less expensive models. It is becoming standard—if the optics aren't waterproof, they are not worth the money.

Does this have a lifetime warranty? Most good binoculars have a good lifetime warranty, even the cheaper ones. If there is no lifetime warranty, it is not worth the price. Also, ask friends with binoculars if they have ever used their warranty and if the service was speedy and prompt.

Is the eye relief adjustable? This is a standard feature on a good set of binoculars. Eyecups can twist out for people without glasses to give them eye relief. People wearing glasses usually do not need the extra relief. Everyone's face is shaped differently, so no one set of eyecups will be comfortable for everyone. That's why trying out binoculars is essential before making a purchase.

Connecting with Other Birders

One of the best ways to improve your birding ability is to go out with other birders, but they may not be easy to find. In some countries, birding is a common practice for people of any age, especially young people. But in the United States, birders are often incorrectly assumed to be the elderly or the nerdiest of the nerdy.

In Central and South America, young people join birding clubs and many grow up to become guides for their country. When they come to the United States to study, they join the local bird club to meet like-minded young people their own age and maybe even a potential date. Many are sorely disappointed to discover that they are the youngest member by thirty years. But it doesn't have to be that way.

Birding with a group is a great way to gain new identification tips and try out new optics.

Travel Tips

The fabulous thing about birding is that it can be done anywhere, even on an afternoon on a business trip in Las Vegas, Nevada. Always at least bring your binoculars.

For some reason, people who engage in this hobby have latched on to unfashionable wear. For years, birders lamented that apart from binoculars, they could not be identified. However the current norm for identifying a birder is a person in ill-fitting khaki clothes that include convertible pants, oversized bird festival shirts, a vest, and floppy hat, which I suppose if you want to concentrate on birds and not be hassled is a great outfit to wear. While I encourage my bird-watching brethren to be prepared for all sorts of weather, dress for comfort and don't be afraid to wear clothing that fits.

Everyone has their secrets on what to pack to make for a perfect birding trip.

If you've never packed for a birding trip, figuring out what to bring can be a daunting task. No matter what I pack for a general area, there are fifteen items that I always bring for birding anywhere in the world at any time of year. This list has never failed me in my travels from Minnesota in winter to Kazakhstan in spring.

Binoculars

Spotting Scope

Camera

Field Guide
(this is getting easier
as more field guides
are available in app form for
smartphones)

Hat
(to provide shade or to
cover up wild hair that comes
with rising at 4 a.m. to
watch grouse at a lek)

Convertible Pants
(they start as pants and
with a quick flick of the wrist,
unzip into shorts)

Light Rain Jacket

Gloves
(no matter what time
of year, you may find yourself
in high elevation and
may have chilly extremities)

Fleece shirt or jacket

Hand Warmers

Bug Spray

Sunscreen

Scarf
(these can provide warmth
around your face and neck, or if
colorful enough, spruce up
your outfit when going to dinner
after a day in the field)

Wool Socks

Waterproof Shoes or Boots

Never pack your optics and camera in checked luggage when flying on a plane. Always find a way to take them as a carry-on. Some tripods can break down and be stowed in carry-on rollaway suitcases but usually are fine if packed in checked luggage. Scopes and binoculars are at risk if sent into checked luggage to be stored under the plane. They can easily disappear, and the airport isn't likely to replace them. Also, if your bag is selected for random inspection, there is no guarantee that the inspector will put them back in the suitcase so they will not get scratched or jostled around. Always pack scopes and binoculars in carry-on luggage. Always.

Backpacks are handy for carry-on luggage. Always keep your binoculars, scope, and camera in your carry-on to guarantee they will arrive safely with you at your birding destination.

BIRD BUSTING!

Never wear white while bird-watching.
No one has taken a formal poll and there's only anecdotal evidence that it bothered one trogon in Arizona. There is something to dressing to disguise yourself in the field, but chances are good that even if you wear camouflaged clothing, the birds can still hear and see you. If you are foolhardy enough to go into the woods during deer season, wear bright orange.

Online Birding

The easiest way for birders to meet up is online through a listserv or forum. A listserv is an online tool where subscribers can send e-mails out to a single address. Every subscriber will receive that e-mail. There are national bird-watching listservs and local ones. Some listservs are only for people who want to know what is rare and unusual showing up for listing purposes, others are friendly general birding forums and people can ask bird feeding questions and share yard observations.

Many sites offer forums, a place where you can ask a question on a bird-watching–related topic and a conversation can start with other members subscribed to the site. This is called a thread, and it's a fun way to meet other birders.

As is possible with any group, e-mail messages can be easily misread and arguments are common when communicating online. Always remember to try to type in a friendly way and read other e-mails from listserv members with a friendly voice.

A simple way to search for a listserv or forum in your area is type the name of your location into a search engine like Google. All it takes is a simple search for "birding" or "bird-watching" or "twitching" to find groups in your area.

There's also the old-fashioned method of joining your local bird club, and there are a few national and even international groups you can check out.

The American Birding Association (ABA) inspires all people to enjoy and protect wild birds. The ABA represents the North American birding community and supports birders through publications, conferences, workshops, tours, partnerships, and networks. It also encourages birders to apply their skills to help conserve birds and their habitats, and they represent the interests of birders in planning and legislative areas. The ABA also sets the standards for watching birds with their ABA Code of Ethics and most birders use the ABA criteria for counting birds on their North American bird list. To learn more visit www.aba.org or find them on Facebook.

The National Audubon Society or Audubon is one of the oldest birding clubs, and though it is interested in protecting several species today, it is popular among birders. Audubon not only is one large national organization, but many states have several smaller chapters and focus almost entirely on bird-watching, offering monthly meetings, newsletters, and frequent bird walks. Learn more at www.Audbubon.org.

The Royal Society for the Protection of Birds is the largest wildlife conservation organization in Europe. They work to protect species and their habitats and offer advice for anyone wishing to make their yards a more wildlife-friendly place.

BirdLife International is a top conservation organization that strives to protect birds and their habitats by working with local communities to build a sustainable partnership.

If you are trying to find local birding clubs online, keep in mind that they can go by many different names from a local Audubon chapter to a society for ornithology. Be sure to try those terms when using an Internet search engine as well as "birding club" and the name of your town or area.

BIRD BUSTING!

Great bird-watching has to be done at the crack of dawn.
No. You can sleep in if you want to. Now it is true that you have more opportunity to see certain species, but if you want to start your bird-watching outing at 10 a.m., that's okay too. As a matter of fact, some bird-watching like hawk-watching doesn't get going until midmorning, so getting up at dawn is a waste.

Smartphones

Technology has changed the birding game in the last few decades. In the 1970s, bird-watchers thought they were on to something by starting phone trees. When a rare bird was reported, people were assigned to call each other to report the rarity. Now, you can literally hold up a smartphone to your spotting scope, get a photo of the bird, email it to your local rare bird committee, or text the photo to a birding friend to make them incredibly jealous.

Short of binoculars and a bottle of water, everything you need for the field can be on the phone: maps, note-taking ability, multiple identification guides, and even the ability to submit your sightings instantaneously to databases like eBird.

Almost all digital identification guides include multiple bird calls and with a quick swipe of the finger, you can play a bird call and get a bird to pop up in easy view, especially when taking photos. However, as we have learned from Spider-Man, "with great power comes great responsibility." Just because we have this power with our phones, should we use it? At this point, there is no firm answer, and if one thing is certain, nothing starts a fight at a bird meeting faster than opening up the debate of using recorded calls to attract birds.

A study of trogons in the late 1970s and early 1980s revealed that playing recorded calls of other trogons did not affect nesting success of breeding pairs. The study suggested that ambient noise from construction did, since the male's song wasn't heard as clearly. A more recent study showed that song sparrows exposed to recorded calls of other males had a spike in testosterone that lasted over twenty-four hours.

A concern shared by many birders is that if a bird is chasing down a phantom rival by being exposed to several taped calls, it is wasting valuable time doing what it should be doing like foraging for food, feeding young, and protecting its nest from predators.

The bottom line is that we do not have enough information to know one way or the other. Some birders would argue that since we do not know, simply do not do play calls. Others would say if it keeps a herd of birders from leaving a trail and crushing a habitat in pursuit of a better view of a rare bird, it's not that bad. Field trip leaders who have been paid money to deliver birds have an expectation to show their clients as many species as possible. If they don't use the calls, they might not be able to stay in business. Some people can mimic several species just by whistling, and many birders are adept at pishing, making sounds that cause birds to pop up.

There is no easy answer. Keep in mind that some public lands like US Fish and Wildlife sites do not allow playing bird calls, and it is illegal and grounds to be thrown out if you are caught. Also some birders have specific personal rules for how they want to count a bird on their list. If you are in a group with other birders and you want to use a recorded call, ask before you play and respect your fellow birders in the field.

THE AMERICAN BIRDING ASSOCIATION
CODE OF ETHICS

This code should be followed in any country.

Everyone who enjoys birds and birding must always respect wildlife, its environment, and the rights of others. In any conflict of interest between birds and birders, the welfare of the birds and their environment comes first.

1. Promote the welfare of birds and their environment.

1(a) Support the protection of important bird habitat.

1(b) To avoid stressing birds or exposing them to danger, exercise restraint and caution during observation, photography, sound recording, or filming.

Limit the use of recordings and other methods of attracting birds, and never use such methods in heavily birded areas, or for attracting any species that is Threatened, Endangered, or of Special Concern, or is rare in your local area;

Keep well back from nests and nesting colonies, roosts, display areas, and important feeding sites. In such sensitive areas, if there is a need for extended observation, photography, filming, or recording, try to use a blind or hide, and take advantage of natural cover.

Use artificial light sparingly for filming or photography, especially for close-ups.

1(c) Before advertising the presence of a rare bird, evaluate the potential for disturbance to the bird, its surroundings, and other people in the area, and proceed only if access can be controlled, disturbance minimized, and permission has been obtained from private land-owners. The sites of rare nesting birds should be divulged only to the proper conservation authorities.

1(d) Stay on roads, trails, and paths where they exist; otherwise keep habitat disturbance to a minimum.

2. Respect the Law, and the rights of others.

2(a) Do not enter private property without the owner's explicit permission.

2(b) Follow all laws, rules, and regulations governing use of roads and public areas, both at home and abroad.

2(c) Practice common courtesy in contacts with other people. Your exemplary behavior will generate goodwill with birders and non-birders alike.

3. Ensure that feeders, nest structures, and other artificial bird environments are safe.

3(a) Keep dispensers, water, and food clean, and free of decay or disease. It is important to feed birds continually during harsh weather.

3(b) Maintain and clean nest structures regularly.

3(c) If you are attracting birds to an area, ensure the birds are not exposed to predation from cats and other domestic animals, or dangers posed by artificial hazards.

4. Group birding, whether organized or impromptu, requires special care.

Each individual in the group, in addition to the obligations spelled out in Items #1 and #2, has responsibilities as a Group Member.

4(a) Respect the interests, rights, and skills of fellow birders, as well as people participating in other legitimate outdoor activities. Freely share your knowledge and experience, except where code 1(c) applies. Be especially helpful to beginning birders.

4(b) If you witness unethical birding behavior, assess the situation, and intervene if you think it prudent. When interceding, inform the person(s) of the inappropriate action, and attempt, within reason, to have it stopped. If the behavior continues, document it, and notify appropriate individuals or organizations. Group Leader Responsibilities [amateur and professional trips and tours].

4(c) Be an exemplary ethical role model for the group. Teach through word and example.

4(d) Keep groups to a size that limits impact on the environment, and does not interfere with others using the same area.

4(e) Ensure everyone in the group knows of and practices this code.

4(f) Learn and inform the group of any special circumstances applicable to the areas being visited (e.g. no tape recorders allowed).

4(g) Acknowledge that professional tour companies bear a special responsibility to place the welfare of birds and the benefits of public knowledge ahead of the company's commercial interests. Ideally, leaders should keep track of tour sightings, document unusual occurrences, and submit records to appropriate organizations.

You can learn more by visiting the ABA website www.aba.org.

Birdfair, Rutland, United Kingdom

Most of the larger birding festivals will have a vending area with reps from different binocular companies, but there's one event that is the largest in the world and it's called Birdfair. This is not a typical birding event in that watching birds is completely secondary. This event happens every August in Rutland, and any company that creates new bird-watching product debuts it here. The event also gathers well-known birders and researchers to give talks during the event. If you are looking for birding guides, spotting scopes, books, or anything related to birds, this is where to go to load up.

Midwest Birding Symposium, Ohio

This event happens every other year on the odd years. There are some bird-watching trips, but most birders attend for the seminars and the chance to check out new product and field guides. The location has switched to several states over the years, but currently the show rests in northern Ohio.

Optics vendors are happy to show you their equipment at shows like Birdfair and the Midwest Birding Symposium.

CHAPTER 10

The Bird-Watching Year

Bird-watching literally can be accomplished every day of the year. If you have a day off and the weather is agreeable to you, you can do it. There are so many places and opportunities; it can be hard to know where to start. Sure, you may hear everyone telling you that Point Pelee is the best bird-watching spot ever, but there are certain times of year that are better than others to get the maximum amount of birds and enjoyment. May is the month when colorful warblers practically drip off of the tree branches. That's not to say you won't get good birds any time of year, but warbler season makes most bird-watchers salivate.

Though common, no one can ever get enough of seeing a great horned owl. As this species learns to adapt to humans, they can just as easily be found in urban areas as in remote wilderness. They are a great example of how cool birds can be found anywhere at anytime, and part of what makes bird-watching so much fun.

Here, I will attempt to give you an idea of events and types of bird-watching to have on your radar for the year. Some of these locations will require a bit of planning and travel but are so worth the destination.

You have two choices for birding early on in the year: go somewhere warm or go for some of those winter specialties. If it's an irruption year, Arctic species will come further south than they usually do, and you get a chance at northern owls, crossbills, redpolls, and grosbeaks. But if you live where winter can last longer than four months, perhaps visiting Central America or anywhere near the equator is more appealing.

The boreal chickadee is a bird that many birders travel to the coldest parts of the United States for, even if it's just a glimpse.

Winter bird-watching is not just for hardcore birders who want to get the most obscure birds on their list as possible; it's a great time to seek out large, easy-to-see birds from the comfort of a toasty warm vehicle while sipping hot chocolate. If you can find areas with open water, you can find bald eagles. Some spots along the upper Mississippi River around Minnesota, Wisconsin, and Iowa will have pockets with dozens, if not hundreds of bald eagles. Even the most jaded nonnature lover cannot help but be impressed by the eagle show in winter.

If you would prefer to watch birds in warmer areas, Florida offers a couple of bird festivals in January. Florida is usually warm and you can tick off quite a few endangered life birds here including wood storks, Florida scrub jays, and red-cockaded woodpeckers.

Also, birds in Florida seem easygoing. Sandhill cranes are a yard bird here and photo opportunities abound with surprisingly cooperative birds. If you want warm weather, fresh seafood, and mellow birds, Florida is the place to be.

Barred antshrikes are a fun Central American bird and one of the many reasons it's fun to see birds in other countries.

Costa Rica, Panama, and Belize are all popular destinations in January. Not only can you view Central American specialties like toucans, forest falcons, and tanagers representing every color of the rainbow, but also it's a chance to glimpse birds that may have been in your backyard in summer like rose-breasted grosbeaks, Baltimore orioles, and painted buntings.

This is actually a good time to visit the Antarctic if you have penguins on your must-see bird list. The days are about as long as they are going to get and penguins will be nesting.

Penguins are not the only birds nesting now. Several owl species start breeding in January, even in northern latitudes. Owls start pairing up in January. If you hear hooting at night, chances are good they are taking over an old hawk nest in your neighborhood.

EVERGLADES BIRDING FESTIVAL

Plantation/Ft. Lauderdale, Florida | www.evergladesbirdingfestival.com

MORRO BAY WINTER BIRD FESTIVAL

Morro Bay, California | www.morrobaybirdfestival.org

SPACE COAST BIRDING AND WILDLIFE FESTIVAL

Titusville, Florida | www.spacecoastbirdingandwildlifefestival.org

WINGS OVER WILLCOX

Willcox, Arizona | www.wingsoverwillcox.com

All of the festivals are great, but the area that I have visited more than once and absolutely love is the Space Coast Birding and Nature Festival. It is one of the largest bird festivals in the country so you can meet bird-watchers of all abilities. There are workshops on photography and this is one of the few bird festivals that will actually take you to a dump in order to hone your gull watching ability. Believe it or not, that trip fills up quickly, so sign up for that early. It's a bit unnerving to see how many birds feed on human trash. Apart from gulls, you will find black and turkey vultures, all manner of herons and egrets, and dozens of the American symbol, the bald eagle.

Because this festival is so huge, it attracts bird vendors from most of the major optics companies as well as many of the best birding tour companies. If you need a new set of binoculars or want to meet some fantastic trip leaders, this is the place go.

Space Coast is also right next to Cape Canaveral, which is an added bonus to the amazing wildlife and birds in January and could be of interest if you are going along with a non-bird-watching companion. You can't go wrong with this festival.

The Florida scrub jay is one of three endangered bird species that can be easily seen at the Space Coast Birding and Wildlife Festival.

FEBRUARY

February is an intense time of year; some areas are in the deepest grips of winter, plunging well below zero degrees Fahrenheit. There aren't many festivals happening, but there is a massive project to get a snapshot view of what is visible in people's backyards called the Great Backyard Bird Count. For four days, people are asked to take a look and note what species and how many there are in their yards. Though most birders do it for an hour or more, it can be for as little as fifteen minutes a day. This is a great project to do with kids and since lists can be submitted online, it's a fun way for them to use a computer.

People may wonder what the big deal about backyard birds is, but it's important to get a snapshot of our common birds and our winter residents. We can see how populations change, who is increasing, and who is decreasing. It's good barometer in case a species is in trouble and needs help. Watching birds for as little as fifteen minutes a day over a period of four days is relatively easy.

Eagles start pairing up in February, and this is a good time to start seeing their mating displays. Eagles will always do touch up on nests throughout the year, but this is the month when serious renovations are underway.

GREAT BACKYARD BIRD COUNT
North America | www.birdsource.org/gbbc

SAX-ZIM BOG BIRDING FESTIVAL
Meadowlands, Minnesota | www.sax-zimbog.com/birding-festival

WHOOPING CRANE FESTIVAL
Port Aransas, Texas | www.whoopingcranefestival.org

This is when we see serious movement of birds and signs of spring. As ponds, lakes, and potholes open up, waterfowl push north. Geese, in particular snow geese, form massive flocks with tens of thousands of birds as they head to their breeding grounds in the Arctic.

March is when several bird species form leks, areas where males display by dancing and fighting to attract females. Find out if your area has a blind or hide that you can check out for a morning to watch this spectacular and sometimes comic display. Though some birds like sharp-tailed grouse and greater and lesser prairie chickens display in a group, others like the ruffed grouse display on their own by drumming their wings while standing on a log.

This is also the month to make sure all of your birding nest boxes are out and ready. You want those wood duck boxes ready at the beginning of the month, but also prepare bluebird, swallow, chickadee, and martin boxes. Those birds will be staking out territory.

Keep an eye out for birds like Stellar's jay in your yard during February's Great Backyard Bird Count.

SAN DIEGO BIRD FESTIVAL

San Diego, California | www.sandiegoaudubon.org/index.php/events/bird-festival

RIVERS AND WILDLIFE CELEBRATION

Kearney, Nebraska | nebraskacranefestival.org

Watching prairie chicken leks are a goal for most birders in the spring. If you can, book time in a blind to watch these crazy birds dance.

This is when migration gets real. Those closer to the Equator get early glimpses of warblers and sparrows returning, while those in northern latitudes anxiously await their arrival.

Savannah sparrows are working their way north, much to the delight of birders anxious for spring.

Lekking birds are still going strong, and there's still plenty of time to catch prairie chicken action and others getting underway like woodcocks. These crazy birds do their display fifteen minutes after sunset and bird-watchers love to partake in watching this ritual as a rite of spring.

There are a plethora of birding festivals and if spring cannot arrive early enough for you, head to Arizona, Florida, or Texas for some fun happy migration times.

Many anxiously await the return of hummingbirds and want to know when to put out their hummingbird feeders. It is said that hummingbirds follow the migration of sapsuckers, eating the sap and small insects that stick to it from the wells the sapsuckers drill. If you see a sapsucker, you could conceivably see a hummingbird.

GALVESTON FEATHERFEST AND NATURE PHOTOFEST

Galveston, Texas | www.galvestonfeatherfest.com

PRAIRIE CHICKEN FESTIVAL

Wisconsin Rapids, Wisconsin | www.prairiechickenfestival.org

GODWIT DAYS SPRING MIGRATION BIRD FESTIVAL

Arcata, California | www.godwitdays.org

POINT REYES BIRDING & NATURE FESTIVAL

Point Reyes Station, California | www.eacmarin.org/point-reyes-birding-festival

DUBOIS GROUSE DAYS

Dubois, Idaho | www.grousedays.org

NEBRASKA PRAIRIE CHICKEN FESTIVAL

Burwell, Nebraska | www.calamusoutfitters.com

FIESTA DE LAS AVES

Bisbee, Arizona | membershipandevents.sabo.org/Fiesta.htm

WHITEFISH POINT SPRING FLING

Paradise, Michigan | www.wpbo.org

LEK TREKS & MORE LESSER PRAIRIE-CHICKEN FESTIVAL

Woodward, Oklahoma | www.lektreks.org

If you have ever considered creating a bird festival or event, avoid the month of May! There is a glut of bird-watching opportunities inside and outside of festivals. Just about everyone has a bird festival and migration is hot and heavy. International Migratory Bird Day falls in May, though everyone seems to host it on a different day. Most birders like to plan their birding in the eastern half of North America to wrack up as many colorful warblers as they can.

However, even if you can only afford to watch birds in your town, you should see loads of them. Check with local parks and nature centers to see if they have trips or events to get the most out of the birds passing through.

The bright blue indigo bunting is a favorite spring bird to seek out.

If just seeing new birds is not enough and you need to get your game on, May is the World Series of Birding, a fundraising competition where birders compete for the most birds seen in one day in Cape May, New Jersey. There are several subcategories like most birds in one county, most birds seen sitting in one spot, and most birds photographed in a day. It's an exhausting event but brings the top birders from around the world.

There's the old wives' tale that now is the time to take in bird-feeding stations because birds will only eat at bird-feeders rather than the abundant natural food surrounding them. It simply is not true and since everyone is breeding, the birds are at their best and brightest. This is an especially fun time to offer grape jelly, orange halves, and nectar for hummingbirds and orioles.

Warblers are what it's all about for many birders in the month of May. Most, like this Wilson's warbler are very bright, though hard to see as they lurk in the leaves.

THE BIGGEST WEEK IN AMERICAN BIRDING
Oregon, Ohio | www.biggestweekinamericanbirding.com

POINT PELEE FESTIVAL OF BIRDS
Leamington, Ontario | Canada | www.friendsofpointpelee.com/festivalofbirds

WINGS OVER THE ROCKIES
Invermere, British Columbia | Canada | www.wingsovertherockies.org

KACHEMAK BAY SHOREBIRD FESTIVAL
Homer, Alaska | www.homeralaska.org/events/kachemakBayShorebirdFestival/index.htm

FERN RIDGE WINGS & WINE FESTIVAL
Veneta, Oregon | www.wingsandwinefestival.com

WORLD SERIES OF BIRDING

Cape May, New Jersey | www.BirdCapeMay.org

WINGS OVER WESTON

Weston, Missouri | www.mostateparks.com/event/59333/wings-over-weston

GREAT SALT LAKE BIRD FESTIVAL

Farmington, Utah | www.greatsaltlakebirdfest.com

KENAI BIRDING FESTIVAL

Kenai Peninsula, Alaska | www.kenaibirdfest.com

DETROIT LAKES FESTIVAL OF BIRDS

Detroit Lakes, Minnesota | www.visitdetroitlakes.com/things-to-do/events/festival-of-birds

SOUTH DAKOTA BIRDING FESTIVAL AT FT. RANDALL

Wagner, South Dakota | www.cityofwagner.org

DORION'S CANYON COUNTRY BIRDING FESTIVAL

Dorion, Ontario, Canada | www.dorionbirdfest.ca

NEW RIVER BIRDING AND NATURE FESTIVAL

Fayetteville, West Virginia | www.birding-wv.com

HORICON MARSH BIRD FESTIVAL

Horicon, Wisconsin | www.horiconmarshbirdfestival.com

ACADIA BIRDING FESTIVAL

Bar Harbor, Maine | www.acadiabirdingfestival.com

Most of May's migrants have settled down into territory and are raising young. Because so many males are still singing on territory, it's a great time to get out and enjoy some bird song. North Dakota prairie is a sublime experience on a June morning. The far northern location can still be cool enough to warrant gloves and a scarf, but sitting in the field at dawn, you will be serenaded by two of the most beautiful birdsongs: the Baird's sparrow and Sprague's pipits.

Though migration is finished, it's a great time to try and see birds as they pair up and raise families. One of the sought-after species in North Dakota during their Potholes and Prairie Bird Festival is the gray partridge.

Even though it's not the busiest time of year, bird banding programs still happen. Check with your local nature center to find one you can observe. Also, this is prime nesting season, see what you can find nesting in your yard and report it to www.nestwatch.org.

POTHOLES & PRAIRIE BIRDING FESTIVAL

Carrington, North Dakota | www.birdingdrives.com

HURON FRINGE BIRDING FESTIVAL

Port Elgin, Ontario | www.friendsofmacgregor.org

LEELANAU PENINSULA BIRDFEST

Lake Leelanau, Michigan | www.mibirdfest.com

YAKUTAT TERN FESTIVAL

Yakutat, Alaska | www.yakutatternfestival.org

GREAT ADIRONDACK BIRDING CELEBRATION

Paul Smiths, New York

www.adirondacklakes.com/recreation/birding/great-adirondack-birding-celebration.html

CERULEAN WARBLER WEEKEND

Hastings, Michigan | www.ceruleanwarbler.org/

ROGER TORY PETERSON BIRDING FESTIVAL

Jamestown, New York | birdfest.rtpi.org

WINGS ACROSS THE BIG SKY

Kalispell, Montana | www.mtaudubon.org/birdwatching/festival.html

Shorebird migration can get an early start, and it is possible to find migratory birds along shores or sod farms. Migration is never truly over.

As far as bird-watching events go, this is one of the quieter times of the year. Though events are happening, if you have bird feeders, it's a great time to watch adults bring their young to feeding stations and teach them how to feed themselves, rather than begging their parents for food.

Many birds like robins, blackbirds, and cardinals might be busy with a second or third nesting attempt, a chance to raise as many young birds as possible. For some, like the American goldfinch, they just start their nesting season now. They wait until the thistle fibers they use to build their nests are available before they lay eggs.

Believe it or not, at the end of July, signs of migration are underway. Sandpipers are migrating, and adults that had failed nests begin to head south. They will always be seen along beaches, but in landlocked areas, look for muddy flats or sod farms for these small birds.

Waterfowl get secretive this time of year as they go through a molt, shed old feathers, and grow in new ones. Several species will be flightless and, therefore, more leery of humans than they would be at other times of the years. Males that have bright, colorful breeding plumage, will be spotty and brown, perhaps an attempt to camouflage while they are flightless during their molt.

Since bird-watching is a little slower this time year, now is a good time to send in binoculars and spotting scopes if they need repair or adjustments. If you try sending them in during spring and fall, you will have a much longer wait because everyone is desperate to have them repaired for migration.

Some species like eastern bluebirds may be on their second or third nesting attempt in your yard at this point.

Though it seems as though birds have just arrived from their spring migration, all too soon it is time for them to head back south.

As hummingbirds begin to gather for migration and the females are teaching their young how to use the feeders, this is one of the best months to attract them.

Shorebirds, nightjars, hummingbirds, and orioles will be the first to go, but hawk, sparrow, and warbler migration will kick in this month too. Bird festival season begins and several areas still offer great bird-watching opportunities.

The largest bird-watching consumer trade show takes places this month in Rutland in the United Kingdom called Birdfair. It is the place to get the latest and greatest in bird tour information, optics, and cameras.

SOUTHWEST WINGS BIRDING AND NATURE FESTIVAL
Sierra Vista, Arizona | swwings.org

BIRDFAIR
Rutland, United Kingdom | www.birdfair.org.uk

TUCSON BIRD & WILDLIFE FESTIVAL
Tucson, Arizona | www.tucsonaudubon.org/festival

TANANA VALLEY SANDHILL CRANE FESTIVAL
Fairbanks, Alaska | www.creamersfield.org

HENDERSON HUMMINGBIRD HURRAH
Henderson, Minnesota | hendersonfeathers.org

Arizona is a great place to visit for a variety of hummingbirds in August. Some bed-and-breakfasts have feeders set out to attract not only birds like this Anna's hummingbird, but birders as well.

Southward migration is full on at this point; many birders particularly enjoy watching hawk migration. In North America, broad-winged hawks and turkey vultures put on quite a show and in some locations, like Hawk Ridge in Minnesota or Hawk Mountain in Pennsylvania, they pass by the thousands overhead.

There's debate that hummingbird feeders should be taken in at this time of year but leave them out, they will be passing through all the way into November and though they will get along fine without your feeder, if you like watching them, enjoy them while you can.

TANANA VALLEY ALASKA SANDHILL CRANE FESTIVAL
Fairbanks, Alaska | www.creamersfield.org

HUMMERBIRD CELEBRATION
Rockport, Texas | www.rockporthummingbird.com

PUGET SOUND BIRD FEST
Edmonds, Washington | www.pugetsoundbirdfest.com

Hawk migration is underway and several species like this merlin will be passing through.

OCTOBER

Migration is still in full swing, though the large numbers of broad-winged hawks are gone, most hawk-watching sites get good numbers of larger birds like red-tailed hawks, bald eagles, northern goshawks and rough-legged hawks. Migratory owls head south and many hawk-watch sites will have nighttime owl banding programs as hundreds of tiny northern saw-whet owls move through.

Areas like Corpus Christi, Texas, and Veracruz, Mexico, will get millions of hawks passing south, and it's a great time to check those migration corridors.

DING DARLING DAYS
Sanibel Island, Florida | www.dingdarlingsociety.org

CAPE MAY AUTUMN BIRDING FESTIVAL
Cape May, New Jersey | www.BirdCapeMay.org

JOHN L. BROOM ALABAMA COASTAL BIRDFEST
Fairhope, Alabama | www.alabamacoastalbirdfest.com

WINGS AND WILDFLOWERS
Tavares, Florida | www.lakecountyfl.com/birding

If you want to visit a festival known as much for the people as the birds, put the Rio Grande Valley Bird Festival on you bucket list. Get great specialties like this great kiskadee and make some birding friends from around the world.

Migration will be winding to a close but it will go out with a bang, as some of the largest birds are the last to move through like sandhill cranes, tundra swans, and bald and golden eagles.

Gulls will also be heading south and hundreds of thousands will gather where there is open water. Hard-core birders love to scan among the masses in the hopes that a rare gull that is out of range will be among them.

There are also birds that come down from the Arctic to spend the winter where winter isn't so bad. Juncos appear at bird feeders, and snow buntings feed along farm roads.

There are still a few bird festivals left to check out for the year, and many birders have their schedules cleared for these events.

COMMON CRANES GATHER IN THE HULA VALLEY IN ISRAEL AND
HULA VALLEY BIRD FESTIVAL
Hula Valley, Israel | www.hulabirdfestival.org

RIO GRANDE VALLEY BIRD FESTIVAL
Harlingen, Texas | www.rgvbf.org

FESTIVAL OF THE CRANES
Bosque Del Apache, New Mexico | www.festivalofthecranes.com

DECEMBER

There's not much going on bird-festival wise in December because of the active holiday season and because it's Christmas Bird Count Season. From December 14 through January 5, Audubon members select a day and try to count as many birds in their assigned area. It's another way of grabbing an idea of what birds are around.

The count started in 1900, and was a protest against the traditional Christmas Day hunts when people would go out and shoot as many birds as possible on Christmas Day. The first count started with twenty-seven observers documenting all the birds they saw and has spread to a nationwide effort today.

Several websites are dedicated to counts and most areas offer more than one over several days, so it's usually very easy to find a count to accommodate your work schedule.

Look up either "Christmas Bird Count" and your city online or get in touch with your local Audobon chapter to learn how you can participate. Even noting the birds at your feeder can help give a snapshot of what birds use your area in winter.

Who knows what you'll see on a Christmas bird count. Maybe you'll find a king eider like this one. These are also a great way to meet other birders.

Ten Areas that Should Be on Every Birders Bucket List

It's perplexing that bird-watching has a somewhat dorky image when this hobby or sport can take you to beautiful landscapes with creatures shaped like what could only come from the imagination of Dr. Seuss. Perhaps birders like to keep it this way so the number of people in the field stays low.

Many birders who travel have their own personal list of where everyone should visit at least once. This is by no means a complete list, but these are places that everyone should consider and strive for at some point, and are definitely worth saving pennies for a trip. That's not to say that if you have an opportunity go bird-watching in Uganda that you will be missing out on something amazing by doing that instead of visiting a cold bog in Minnesota, but these are areas that you will hear lots of birders talk about with reverence.

10. CANOPY TOWER, PANAMA

This is an area that you will see advertised in lots of magazines and almost every professional birding tour company offers a tour to this place. Canopy Tower Family owns several lodgings, but the most popular is Canopy Tower, a converted military observation tower. The barracks have been converted into rooms; the upper floor is a common area with hammocks, books, windows, and beverages served throughout the day. The top floor deck is what people are really after.

The deck offers a 360-degree view. In one direction, you see Panama City in the distance; in another, the famed Panama Canal and everything else is forest. In the evening, you can sip a cocktail as bat falcons soar overhead hawking insects and listen to plaintive infamous, monstrous-sounding howler monkeys, and the harsh caw of a collared forest falcon in the distance.

The company employs professional local guides, so even if you purchase a visit on your own, you will be in capable hands. The moonwalking birds or red-capped manakins

can be found on the walk down the driveway and nighttime tours will show you potoos, sloths, and coatis.

Keep in mind that this was meant for barracks and sound travels easily through the tower. This is not a recommended honeymoon spot, as your neighbors will hear everything. For that, check into the Canopy Lodge, a luxurious open-air lodge in higher elevations with an outdoor library and a banana bird feeder that attracts tanagers, euphonies, and orioles and has a resident motmot to greet you in the morning.

This is a popular destination in winter but if you go in the off-season during summer, prices will be cheaper. If hawk migration trips your trigger, book time at the tower between mid-September and mid-December and watch millions of hawks and vultures zip south into South America.

Based on Israel's location in the Middle East and position next to the Mediterranean Sea, many migratory birds get funneled through here. Thousands of storks, cranes, herons, and kites can be seen when the winds are right in the spring and fall.

However, November is the best month for the spectacular common crane migration. Tens of thousands of cranes stop in the valley to fuel up for their migration, however, in recent years, roughly thirty thousand spend the winter there. Since farming happens year-round in this temperate region, there have been some strategies employed by the government to help the farms and provide a remarkable bird-watching tourism opportunity.

Cranes are allowed to feed on discarded seeds in certain fields, funded by the government. When the cranes wander into fields that are used for farming, hired bird- scarers drive out and shoot guns and fireworks to get the cranes to flush. The birds soon figure out which fields are quiet and which ones to avoid. Because the birds are used to seeing farm equipment like tractors, the Agamon Hula Nature Reserve will take visitors out in mobile hides attached to the back of tractors and you can get astoundingly close views of the cranes. The cranes are used to the machinery and casually walk out of the way. While on the tractors, you will also see jungle cats, jackals, black francolins, crested larks, greater spotted eagles, pallid harriers, and stone chats.

The Hula is an easy distance from Mount Hermon, which offers spectacular views of Israel and the surrounding countries of Lebanon and Syria. If you stay awhile, you can also take a few days to go down to the Negev to see cream-colored coursers, red-footed falcons, squacco heron, and long-legged buzzards.

If you live in the Americas, Israel is an ideal place to add a great mix of species to your list since they get birds from Europe, Asia, and Africa. You got a great variety for your tourism dollar. Almost everyone speaks English, and it is incredibly safe to visit. Although hiring a guide to find birds is best, most places are safe and easily accessible on your own.

There are at least two bird festivals in Israel and one specifically for crane-watching every November.

Thousands of cranes are the main reason to go to northern Israel, but the landscape is also breathtaking.

If you would like to get a sense of what it's like to be the last person on Earth, Kazakhstan's vast landscapes will do it for you. This large country offers both short grass prairie habitat and mountainous views, and if you can, explore as much of it as you can possibly afford. However, if you can only get to one spot, the Tien Shan Mountains will wow you with their beauty and the crazy bird life hidden in their heights.

A trip in May will surround you with the haunting wails of the Himalayan snowcock echoing off the cliffs and the cheerful warbles of the Himalayan rubythroat on the surrounding boulders. A walk around the reservoir could get you views of the ibisbill, hobbies, fire-fronted serins, and if you can make it up to the abandoned research station, you could glimpse the tit-warbler, a tiny purple-and-blue bird hidden in the brush.

Keep an eye open on the terrain. Some jokesters have created a huge Batman insignia by arranging boulders on the side of the mountain. Western pop culture is inescapable.

This Himalayan rubythroat is a cheery singer that lurks among the boulders in the Tien Shan Mountains.

One cannot think of the Rio Grande Valley without thinking of the green jay, one of the most common feeder birds to come into backyards.

7. RIO GRANDE VALLEY, TEXAS

This part of south Texas is so close to the Mexican border and is a fantastic birding destination. It's close to two international airports and if you stay in the smaller towns of McAllen, Texas, or Harlingen, Texas, the lodging and food rates are incredibly low.

This area is prized because so many Mexican specialties creep up into the United States border, and it's a great way to inflate your North American bird list. Rainbow-colored green jays, pyrrhuloxias, clay-colored thrushes, and buff-bellied hummingbirds are common feeder birds and large, boisterous plain chachalacas lurk among the shrubs. Surprises always pop up like brown jays, rose-throated becards, and golden-crowned warblers. Driving around town, you may see tropical kingbirds, great kiskadees, and red-naped parrots. Being close to the border gives you access to all kinds of authentic Mexican food, and since it's so close to South Padre Island, even a nonbirding partner can find things to do while you bird-watch to your heart's content among palm trees or over beaches.

One of the older and most popular bird festivals takes place every November called the Rio Grande Valley Bird Festival and attracts top birders as guides and participants year after year. South Texas can be visited at any time so if you cannot make the festival itself, all the bird-watching tour companies lead tours to the areas and there are several local guides for hire. The area is so well known that it is easy enough to visit parks and get your target species.

6. PRIBILOF ISLANDS, ALASKA

Many birders have Alaska on their list, but if you are going to go up there, you might as well go whole hog and make a point of heading to the Pribilof Islands, a group of volcanic islands that are as far west of Alaska as you can go, and is a mere five hundred miles from the Siberian Coast.

The appeal of these remote islands are all the Siberian rarities that can show up, as well as up-close views of thousands of nesting birds like horned and tufted puffins, common murres, red-faced cormorants, and northern fulmars.

This is another area that will make you feel like the last person on Earth. Unlike other places that are ready for nature tourism, the accommodations may not be luxurious but you could be rewarded with some of the most uncommon birds on your United States bird list.

5. PLATTE RIVER, NEBRASKA

March in Nebraska is one of the true wonders of the world and millions of birds use the Platte River and surrounding fields full of waste corn to bulk up for their northward migration to the Arctic. If you visit in early March, you can find over a million snow geese. The birds are so thick, they can be mistaken for snow covering fields or ice coating a reservoir. When the birds are frightened, they ascend into the air, forming a giant tornado of birds, with a din that can be heard for miles.

Thousands of sandhill cranes will be present but their numbers increase in mid-March. Rowe Sanctuary offers morning and evening blind viewing tours and everyone has a favorite. When you arrive in the morning, you are instructed to sit in silence in the dark. You can hear that there are thousands of cranes out on the water and as light gradually increases, you can see thousands of cranes on the islands. Eventually when dawn is bright and perfect for photos, a coyote will run by or a bald eagle will fly over, scaring the cranes and the flock will lift into the air. You realize that the cranes were not on islands. There were so many birds packed into one spot on the river, it looked like an island. Each individual crane's cry merges with thousands of others into one large scream, and the sound is so great, you cannot hear your own thoughts. The flock is so massive that it forms a cloud in the sky.

There is a Rivers and Wildlife Celebration that happens in March and offers not only crane-viewing opportunities but also visits to greater prairie chicken leks and daylong fieldtrips to view migrating ducks in potholes around the region. Do whatever you can to raise the funds, but find a way to get to Nebraska in March.

That's not ice on Harlan Reservoir in Nebraska; that's a million snow geese.

A cold morning in Nebraska watching 40,000 sandhill cranes is an unforgettable experience. If you go in early March, you might get a million snow geese too.

4. BIRDFAIR, UNITED KINGDOM

This isn't exactly a destination for birds, but this is the largest consumer show for birders in the world. The latest in bird-watching gear from optics to gadgets to books are found here often before they are found anywhere else. Birdfair also brings in guest speakers, authors, and TV personalities for lectures and programs.

The truly amazing part of the festival is not the gathering of birders and twitchers and top birding gear, but it's the tremendous amount of fundraising for wildlife raised by the event. There's a different fundraising theme every year and in 2011, Birdfair raised almost £250,000 ($307,000 USD) for endemic birds in Ethiopia.

Birdfair happens every year in August and though there are others, none compare in size to the British version.

3. SAX-ZIM BOG, MINNESOTA

The appeal of this tamarack bog is that it is relatively close to major international airports with Minneapolis and St. Paul only three hours away.

This bog has the potential for birders to load up on their northern species like great gray owls, northern hawk owls, northern goshawks, black-backed and three-toed woodpeckers, boreal chickadees, pine and evening grosbeaks, common and hoary redpolls, gray jays, and spruce grouse.

The best way to do the bog is to hire a guide, but many people arm themselves with books and postings from the local listserv and drive the roads hoping to come up on owls. Though some residents in the bog prefer birders not to aim their binoculars at their home, a few set up birdfeeders at the ends of their driveways along with a donation box, and it's an easy and fun way to see your winter finches and grosbeaks, as well as a great opportunity for photographers to get souvenir shots of birds.

There's a small festival in the winter but guides can be hired at any time of year. Guides are an especially good idea if you are not used to driving on snow- and ice-covered gravel roads. Though the bog is most prized for the northern winter birds, it's great bird-watching in summer with the potential for yellow rails and Connecticut warblers.

2. FLORIDA COAST

Birds in Florida are very laid-back. It's quite interesting to note the difference in behavior. If you take a moment to look at a sandhill crane in Wisconsin, it will fly away as fast as it can. In Florida, they are yard birds. Even secretive bitterns seem fine with you pausing for several moments to take their photos. I've even seen bitterns pose to their left and after you took all the photos you thought you needed, shift to give you a look at their right side.

Florida has so many areas that are perfect for bird-watching and photography. Some might argue that the Space Coast on the east side near Cape Canaveral is the best spot but once you go to Sanibel, you don't go back.

Sanibel Island is just off the Gulf Coast and hosts Ding Darling National Wildlife Refuge, a bird photographer's dream. Coastal species like anhingas, little blue herons, roseate spoonbills, and glossy ibises all pose in the gorgeous sun. There are also barred owls, red-shouldered hawks, and osprey ready to snap. Florida is another great compromise for going out with a non-bird-watching partner—there's always agreement when it come to a beach vacation.

Visiting Florida will not only show you crazy birds that look like Dr. Seuss characters like roseate spoonbills and white ibises, but you'll notice the birds are mellow and accustomed to voyeurs.

1. GALÁPAGOS ISLANDS, SOUTH AMERICA

Anyone remotely interested in wildlife, natural history, or biology has the Galápagos Islands on their bucket list. For many birders, this is the end all, be all since you can get up-close looks at blue-footed boobies and flightless cormorants. Other amazing species include red-billed tropic birds, swallow-tailed gulls, Darwin's finch, great frigatebirds, and the Galápagos hawk.

These islands are only accessible by boat and many bird-watching companies offer tours. If bird-watching is your preferred area of study, definitely make a point to go with a bird-themed tour. These islands offer so much to learn that going with a marine biology expert may not get you the bird experience you would like. Rest assured that if you go with a bird-themed tour, you would still get a chance to view marine iguanas and seals.

This is a basic list. What additions would you make? Have you found areas to visit? The important thing to remember is that you can do this; it can be as casual or intense as you wish it to be.

Go out. Watch birds. Your adventure awaits.

Appendix

Glossary
(aka weird things you might hear birders say)

Accidental: A bird that is not supposed to be on a specific continent. If you go by the American Birding Association Guidelines, an "Accidental Species" is even more unusual than a "Rare Species." Yes, it is somewhat confusing.

Accipiter: Hawks are in the genus accipiter. Many look alike and are tough to identify. When a smallish hawk with short wings and a long tail flies by or ambushes birds, you will often hear a birder say, "There's an accipiter!"

Aerie: A nest on the side of a cliff or mountain usually associated with birds of prey like a golden eagle.

Air Sac: Small sacs around a bird's body that work with the lungs as their respiratory system.

Albino: A bird that is completely lacking in pigment in its entire body. The bird's feathers will be white while its skin, eyes, and other tissue will be pink. Albinos are all or nothing. Some birds will have regular plumage and a few all-white feathers, that is not partial albinism, that is a bird that has a few feathers lacking pigment.

Alternate Plumage: This is another term for birds that grow in brighter feathers for the breeding season. Some might call this breeding plumage, but a birder who wishes to sound cool among other birding folk would say alternate plumage.

Altitudinal Movement: Birds who migrate to different elevations on a mountain rather than latitudinal movement like robins and warblers.

Altricial: A fancy word for naked chicks or baby birds that hatch from the shell blind, featherless and helpless. They are unable to leave the nest or move and rely on adults for survival. This can also be referred to as nidicolous.

Arboreal: A bird that lives in a tree, believe it or not, some birds don't fancy trees.

Auriculars: Feathers around a bird's ear.

Axilliaries: Feathers on the underside of a bird's wing.

Basic Plumage: A bird's winter plumage.

Bat: Not a bird but a flying mammal and many people will assume you know lots about them if you are into birds.

Beak: The usually pointy thing on the front of a bird's face. Also called a bill.

Buteo: This is the genus of hawks that includes red-tailed hawks and common buzzards. They are large, chunky hawks with fat broad wings and a short tail. When a birder sees a hawk and is uncertain of the exact species, they might say, "Large buteo banking to the northeast."

Cere: What birds have for a nose, it's the notch at the base of the bill with two nostrils in it.

Clutch: The total number of eggs in a nest in one cycle. If a clutch is lost, a female may lay another or in the case of some species like robins, they may raise several clutches in a breeding season.

Colonial: Birds that nest in a group like house sparrows or purple martins.

Congeneric: Birds that are separate species but in the same genus. For example red-billed chough and alpine choughs are separate species, but are in the same genus.

Conspecific: A fancy way of saying birds that are members of the same species. An example would be: American coots reproduction involves a lot of conspecific brood parasitism, meaning female American coots are laying eggs in other American coot nests.

Coverts: Coverts can be on the wing or above the tail. They are the short feathers that cover longer feathers.

Creche: A group of fledging birds that form in nesting colonies for species like penguins, ostriches, or flamingos. They are still tended by adults. These can also be referred to as pods.

Crepuscular: Birds that are active at dawn and dusk.

Crissum: Fluffy feathers that hide a bird's naughty bits. Also referred to as undertail coverts.

Crop: A pouch in the esophagus that acts as a food storage area for many bird species. Some birds can have such a large crop that it gives what's known as the "Dolly Parton Effect" to their chest area.

Crown: The top of a bird's head.

Culmen: The top ridge of the upper mandible of a bird's beak. You would be surprised how often this word comes up in identification conversations.

Dabbling: Used when referring to ducks that feed from the top of a water's surface, tipping their butts up in the air as they dip below to gain access to food and invertebrates.

Decurved: A description of a bird bill that slopes downward.

Dihedral: A smart-sounding word that means a bird is holding its wings in a "V shape" while gliding or soaring.

Diurnal: Active during the day.

Divers: This word can either refer to loons or to several species of fish eating ducks that dive below the water's surface to hunt for prey.

Eclipse Plumage: A weird little plumage that male ducks molt into usually in midsummer. They are flightless and must hide from predators. They tend to look like the female of their species, as browns and grays make hiding much easier. If it's midsummer and you aren't seeing any mallards, it's probably a total eclipse of the duck and they are hiding.

Egg: The place where baby birds come from, deposited by female birds.

Empid: An abbreviated version of the genus empidonax, a vexing group of birds that look very much alike and in some regions at the right time of year cannot be easily identified. If you want to sound smart and you see a flycatcher, simply say, "Huh, we have an empid at about two o'clock in that tree," and then wait and see who has the cojones to try and identify it. Another all too common phrase is, "Darn empids!"

Extirpated: A bird that has been driven out of its previous range. Barn owls are extirpated in Minnesota. They used to be there, but their range no longer includes that state.

Feaking: A falconry term referring to when a raptor wipes its beak off on a perch, but if you watch birds long enough, several species do this.

Ferruginous: Having a reddish-brown or rusty colored appearance to the feathers.

Field Marks: Feathers, colors, patterns, or any physical feature that identifies a specific species.

Fledgling: A young bird that is leaving the nest and learning to fly or run. This can also be a verb if you watch a young cardinal leave the nest for the first time you could tell someone, "That baby cardinal fledged today!"

Fright Molt: Birds will drop several feathers under extreme stress, like when grabbed by a raptor. Losing a tail and having a tough time ruddering while flying is a better price to pay than being dead an eaten.

Frugivorous: Birds that prefer to eat fruit.

Gonys: The area on the lower half of a gull's mandible. Many species have a red spot on it.

Gorget: Chin area on a male hummingbird that flashes with colorful feathers.

Gular Sac: A pouch on the throat of a bird that is sometimes used to maintain body temperature. When an owl is panting while hot, it is engaged in gular fluttering. Male magnificent frigatebirds have a gigantic gular pouch that is used in their mating displays.

Hallux: The toe that faces backward on most birds.

Hawking: If a falconer is using this term, they are going hunting with their raptor. Birders use this to refer to birds like flycatchers or Lewis's woodpeckers that fly out from a perch and catch an aerial insect.

Immature: A bird that has not reached adult plumage but is no longer in the juvenal plumage.

Juvenal Plumage: First feather plumage grown by baby birds. Some species lose this plumage quickly; others will retain it for a year.

Juvenile Bird: This is a bird still in its juvenal plumage.

Lamellae: Tiny ridges along the bill of waterfowl like ducks and swans that allow them to filter out water when they have a beakful of food.

Larder: Food storage areas, usually applied to shrikes or acorn woodpeckers.

Lek: A dancing ground where several males will come together to display for females.

Leucistic: A bird that has plumage that appears unusually pale or extremely washed out.

Lores: The tiny spaces between the eyes and base of the bill on a bird's head. Take a look at a white-throated sparrow, they have yellow lores.

Malar Stripe: Generally applied to the dark mark under the eyes of falcons.

Mantling: The act of a bird of prey like a hawk or eagle when it puffs up its feathers and extends its wings over food.

Master Cock: In the Hall of Worst Scientific Names, this one takes the cake. It is the dominant male on a lek. Do not be alarmed if you are out in the Nebraska sandhills and watching prairie chickens dance and you hear an ornithologist say, "Oh, hey, that must be the master cock." Stand down the pepper spray.

Melanistic: A bird that has darker feathers than the more commonly seen plumage.

Molt: The process a bird goes through to shed old feathers and grow in new ones. Some birds molt several times a year while others molt about once a year.

Morph: Some birds of the same species can have different plumage colors. Once a bird grows into its color morph, it will stay that color the rest of its life. For example, snow geese come in two color morphs, white and blue. Since they are the same species, both color morphs will mate with each other.

Neotropical: This term is applied to birds that breed in the United States and Canada but migrate into Central and South America.

New World Species: Means birds found in the Western Hemisphere and includes North, Central, and South America.

Nocturnal: Active at night.

Nonpasserine: These are nonperching birds like waterfowl, birds of prey, shorebirds, waders, woodpeckers, and doves.

Old-World Species: Means birds found in the Eastern Hemisphere and includes Europe, Asia and Africa.

Palearctic: The northern half of the globe east of the Prime Meridian—from the northern part of the Sahara in Africa, the central part of the Arabian Peninsula, and the foothills of the Himalayan Mountains in Asia to the Arctic region in Russia. Area surrounded by the Arctic, Atlantic, and Pacific Oceans.

Passerine: This refers to perching birds like robins, cardinals, warblers, and chickadees.

Peep: A collective term for tiny shorebirds that look remarkably similar unless you are some sort of avian savant. The name comes from the peep sound given as the birds fly away for the desperate observer. Common sentence usage, "Did anyone see a white rump on one of those peeps in that flock that flew away?"

Pelagic: This is used to refer to birds that spend most of their time over large bodies of water like the ocean, sea, or great lakes. Pelagic bird-watching trips involve taking daylong trips out over open water to search for jaegers, albatross, petrels . . . and a fair amount of nausea.

Pied: A bird that has normal coloration in the feathers, but some feathers are white, giving it a patchy appearance.

Plumage: The colors and pattern in feathers that cover and identify a bird.

Polyandrous: Females who have more than one mate.

Polygynous: Males who have more than one mate.

Preening: The action of a bird using its bill to maintain its feathers. The process involves using its beak to excrete oils from its preen gland and then going over each feather.

Primaries: The longer feathers on the outer tips of a bird's wings.

Primary Projection: This refers to how far the primaries (the longest wing tip feathers) stick out from the longest tertials on the wing. Birders love to argue this identification feature for hours.

Raptors: Generally applied to birds of prey that grab and kill things with their toes. This used to include new world vultures, but they don't kill with their feet. Some places still consider them raptors.

Remiges: An impressive way to say "flight feathers."

Retrices: A fancy word for tail feathers.

Rouse: This is when a bird raises all its feathers and shakes them vigorously to put them all back into place.

Scapulars: A cool way to refer to shoulder feathers.

Secondaries: Feathers on the wing between the primaries and the tertiaries (the feathers in the middle).

Semipalmated: Birds that have toes that are partially webbed.

Speculum: No ladies, it's not what you think when it comes to birds. In birding terms it's the patch of iridescent feathers on duck wings.

Supercilium: The line above each eye, a sort of eyebrow.

Tarsus: The top of a bird's foot behind the toes.

Tertials: Wing feathers closest to the body.

Vent: The butt of the bird where the excrement comes out.

Wing: Appendages covered with feathers that allow most birds to fly. Some wings are more functional than others.

Bibliography

Don't just think of this as a list of resources used for this book, but as a suggested reading list. My hope is that reading this book will spark more of an interest in birds and that you will want to go out and learn more. Go, read, and learn from these other great books and online resources. They are organized into birding interest level. I would hate for you to be all excited about birds and then pick for your second birding tome a big book about molt. Though that is an exciting book in its own right, it might be intimidating for someone who just wants to know more about those red birds in the back yard.

BEGINNER

Attenborough, David. *The Life of Birds*. Princeton, NJ: Princeton University Press, 1998.

Elliot, Lang. *Music of the Birds, A Celebration of Bird Song*. New York: Houghton Mifflin Company, 1999.

Hill, Geoffrey E. *National Geographic Bird Coloration*. Washington D.C.: National Geographic Society, 2010.

Oddie, Bill. *Bill Oddie's Little Black Bird Book*. London: Anova Books, 2006.

Poole, Robert M. ed. *The Wonder of Birds*. Washington D.C.: National Geographic Society, 1983.

Proctor, Noble S., and Lynch, Patrick J. *Manual of Ornithology, Avian Structure & Function*. New Haven: Yale University, 1993.

Stiteler, Sharon, *City Birds Country Birds: How Can Anyone Attract Birds to Their Feeder*. Cambridge, MN: Adventure Publications, 2008.

Thompson, Bill III ed. *Identify Yourself: The 50 Most Common Birding Identification Challenges*. Boston: Houghton Mifflin Company, 2005.

Unwin, Mike. *The Atlas of Birds: Diversity, Behavior, and Conservation*. Princeton, NJ: Princeton University Press, 2011.

Weidensaul, Scott. *Living on the Wind: Across the Hemisphere with Migratory Birds*. New York: North Point Press, 2000.

Wells, Diana. *100 Birds and How They Got Their Names*. Chapel Hill: Algonquin Books of Chapel Hill, 2002

KNOWS MORE THAN THE AVERAGE BEAR

Beletsky, Les. *Global Birding*. Washington D.C.: National Geographic Society, 2010.

Bird, David M. *The Bird Almanac*. Revised and Updated. Buffalo, Firefly Books, 2004.

Choate, Ernest A. *The Dictionary of American Bird Names, Revised Edition*. Boston: The Harvard Common Press, 1985.

Goodfellow, Peter. *Avian Architecture: How Birds Design, Engineer & Build*. Princeton, NJ: Princeton University Press, 2011.

Heinrich, Bernd. *Mind of the Raven*. New York: Cliff Street Books, 1999.

Kaufman, Kenn. *Advanced Birding*. Boston: Houghton Mifflin Company, 1990.

Redig, Patrick T., Tordoff, Harrison B. "Peregrine Falcon Reintroduction in the Upper Mississippi Valley and Western Great Lakes Region" *Peregrine Falcon Populations Their Management and Recovery* (1988) 52: pp. 559-63.

Todd, Frank S. *10,001 Titillating Tidbits of Avian Trivia*. Vista: Ibis Publishing Company, 1994.

Weidensaul, Scott. *Of a Feather: A Brief History of American Birding*. San Diego: Harcourt Inc., 2007.

Young, Jon. *What The Robin Knows*. New York: Houghton Mifflin Harcourt, 2012.

HARD-CORE MAXI BIRD BOOKS

Elbroch, Mark, Marks, Eleanor. *Bird Tracks & Sign*. Mechanicsburg, Pa.: Stackpole Books, 2001.

Howell, Steve N. G. *Peterson Reference Guide to Molt in North American Birds*. New York: Houghton Mifflin Harcourt, 2010.

Pyle, Peter. *Identification Guide to North American Birds Parts I & II*. Ann Arbor: Braun-Brumfield Inc., 1997 & 2008

Scott, David S., McFarland, Casey. *Bird Feathers*. Mechanicsburg: Stackpole Books, 2010.

ARTICLES AND ONLINE RESOURCES

"All About Birds." The Cornell Lab of Ornithology. http://www.allaboutbirds.org.

Associated Press. "Museum experts ID birds that bring down planes," by Michael Tarm, Phys.org, June 14, 2009, http://phys.org/news164164818.html.

Auman, Heidi J., Ludwig, James P., Giesy, John P., and Colborn, Theo. "Plastic ingestion by Laysan Albatross chicks on Sand Island, Midway Atoll, in 1994 and 1995." *Albatross Biology and Conservation* (1997): pp. 239–44.

Birds of North America Online. https://bna.birds.cornell.edu/bna.

Driscoll, Emily V. "Bisexual Species: Unorthodox Sex in the Animal Kingdom." *Scientific American Online*. July 10, 2008. http://www.scientificamerican.com/article.cfm?id=bisexual-species

Ehrlick, Paul R., Dobkin, David S., and Wheye, Darryl. "Copulation" and "Polyandry in the Spotted Sandpiper." Stanford. 1988. http://www.stanford.edu/group/stanfordbirds/text/essays/Copulation.html

Ehrlick, Paul R., Dobkin, David S., and Wheye, Darryl. "Polyandry in the Spotted Sandpiper." Stanford. 1988. http://www.stanford.edu/group/stanfordbirds/text/essays/Polyandry_in_the_Spotted.html.

Goudarzi, Sara. "Homosexual Animals Out of the Closet." Live Science. November 16, 2007. http://www.livescience.com/1125-homosexual-animals-closet.html.

Hansford, Dave, "Alaska Bird Makes Longest Flight Ever Measured." *National Geographic Online*. September 14, 2007. http://news.nationalgeographic.com/news/2007/09/070913-longest-flight.html.

Julie Zickefoose Blog, "Zick Dough Improved," blog entry by Julie Zickefoose, March 7, 2010. http://juliezickefoose.blogspot.com/2010/03/zick-dough-improved.html.

Kessler, Rebecca, "Why It's OK for Birds to Be Gay." Live Science. August 23, 2010. http://www.livescience.com/11125-birds-gay.html.

Kuwae, T., Miyoshi, E., Hosokawa, S., Ichimi, K., Hosoya, J., Amano, T., Moriya, T., Kondoh, M., Ydenberg, R. C. and Elner, R. W. "Variable and complex food web structures revealed by exploring missing trophic links between birds and biofilm." *Ecology Letters* (2012) 15 pp. 347–356.

Leggett, Hadley, "Toucan Beak Is New Kind of 'Heating Bill.'" *Wired Online*. July 23, 2009. http://www.wired.com/wiredscience/2009/07/toucanbill

MacLeod, Donald, "Necrophilia among ducks ruffles research feathers," *The Guardian Online*. March 8, 2005. http://www.guardian.co.uk/education/2005/mar/08/highereducation.research.

McClain, Joseph, "Two tracked whimbrels survive storms only to die of gunfire." College of William and Mary. September 13, 2011. http://www.wm.edu/news/stories/2011/machi-the-whimbrel-survives-hurricanes-to-die-of-gunfire-123.php.

Owen, James, "Coot Birds Can Count, Study Says." *National Geographic Online*. April 2, 2003. http://news.nationalgeographic.com/news/2003/04/0402_030402_coots.html.

Pearson, Helen, "Birds feel the rub," *Nature Online*. July 16, 2001. doi:10.1038/news010719-4. http://www.nature.com/news/2001/010716/full/news010719-4.html.

McKenna, Phil, "Good vibrations get a club-winged manakin going." *New Scientist Online*. November 11, 2009. http://www.newscientist.com/article/dn18130-good-vibrations-get-a-clubwinged-manakin-going.html.

Milius, Susan, "When Birds Divorce." *Science News Online*. March 7, 1998. http://www.science-news.org/pages/sn_arc98/3_7_98/bob1.htm.

Mooallem, Jon. "Can Animals Be Gay." *The New York Times Online*, March 31, 2010. https://www.nytimes.com/2010/04/04/magazine/04animals-t.html?_r=1&pagewanted=all.

Powell, Hugh, "The Case of the Bizarre Beaks." *Living Bird Online*, (Winter 2011). http://www.allaboutbirds.org/page.aspx?pid=2137.

Reuters, "Duck penises show battle of the sexes," by Maggie Fox, ABC Science, May 1, 2007, http://www.abc.net.au/science/articles/2007/05/01/1911284.htm.

Salleh, Anna, "Found! The longest bird penis ever." ABC Science. September 14, 2001. http://www.abc.net.au/science/articles/2001/09/14/366856.htm.

Science Alert, "Birds refute monogamy theory." *Science Alert Online*. November 24, 2009. http://www.sciencealert.com.au/news-nz/20092411-20289.html.

Science Alert, "New research helps ostriches orgasm." *Science Alert Online*. May 14, 2008. http://www.sciencealert.com.au/news/20081505-17323-2.html.

Science Daily, "Polygamy, Paternal Care in Birds Linked to Dinosaur Ancestry." *Science Daily Online*. December 19, 2008. http://www.sciencedaily.com/releases/2008/12/081218141734.htm.

United States Geological Survey, "Migration of Birds: Flight Speed and Rate of Migration." Northern Prairie Wildlife Research Center. http://www.npwrc.usgs.gov/resource/birds/migratio/speed.htm.

Weaver, Janelle. "Parental Care Linked To Homosexuality." *Nature Online*. July 9, 2010. http://www.nature.com/news/2010/100709/full/news.2010.344.html.

Photo Credits

All the photographs are by the author except as noted below and are used by permission.

Photos on pages 8 (third down), 42 by Randall Kinkor.

Photos on pages 12, 54 & 178 by Larry Sirvio.

Photos on pages 18, 22, 40, 46, 123 & 154 by Richard Phillips.

Photos on pages19, 41, 47, 62 & 88, by Michele Dupraw.

Photos on page 35 by Jay Ovsiovitch.

Photos on pages 48 & 122 by Matt Bango.

Photos on page 57 by Linda Munson.

Photos on pages 60 & 243 by Richard Dupraw.

Photos on pages 66, 94, 96 & 108 by Craig Nash.

Photos on pages 73 & 109 by Julia Waters.

Photos on pages 112 & 144 by Mike Watson.

Photo on page 117 by Jason Frederick.

Photos on page 130 by Kenneth Herdy.

Photo on page 147 by Peter Jones.

Photo on page 149 by Judy Watson.

Photo on page 155 by Susanne Stam.

Photo on page 174 by Frank Taylor.

Photo on page 185 by Craig A. Mullenbach.

Photos on page 189 by Peter Perrino.

Photo on page 205 by Dave Magpiong.

Photo on page 223 by Amy Hooper.

Photos on pages 238 & 250 by Dan Arndt.

Photo on page 252 by Julie Waters.

Index

Italicized numbers indicate a photograph.